teach yourself

special forces

teach yourself®

special forces
anthony kemp

For over 60 years, more than 40 million people have learnt over 750 subjects the **teach yourself** way, with impressive results.

be where you want to be with **teach yourself**

For UK order enquiries: please contact Bookpoint Ltd, 130 Milton Park, Abingdon, Oxon OX14 4SB. Telephone: +44 (0) 1235 827720. Fax: +44 (0) 1235 400454. Lines are open 09.00–18.00, Monday to Saturday, with a 24-hour message answering service. Details about our titles and how to order are available at www.teachyourself.co.uk

For USA order enquiries: please contact McGraw-Hill Customer Services, PO Box 545, Blacklick, OH 43004-0545, USA. Telephone: 1-800-722-4726. Fax: 1-614-755-5645.

For Canada order enquiries: please contact McGraw-Hill Ryerson Ltd, 300 Water St, Whitby, Ontario L1N 9B6, Canada. Telephone: 905 430 5000. Fax: 905 430 5020.

Long renowned as the authoritative source for self-guided learning – with more than 40 million copies sold worldwide – the **teach yourself** series includes over 300 titles in the fields of languages, crafts, hobbies, business, computing and education.

British Library Cataloguing in Publication Data: a catalogue record for this title is available from the British Library.

Library of Congress Catalog Card Number: on file.

First published in UK 2004 by Hodder Arnold, 338 Euston Road, London, NW1 3BH.

First published in US 2004 by Contemporary Books, a Division of the McGraw-Hill Companies, 1 Prudential Plaza, 130 East Randolph Street, Chicago, IL 60601 USA.

This edition published 2004.

The **teach yourself** name is a registered trade mark of Hodder Headline Ltd.

Copyright © 2004 Anthony Kemp

Typeset by Transet Limited, Coventry, England.
Printed in Great Britain for Hodder Arnold, a division of Hodder Headline, 338 Euston Road, London NW1 3BH, by Cox & Wyman Ltd, Reading, Berkshire.

Hodder Headline's policy is to use papers that are natural, renewable and recyclable products and made from wood grown in sustainable forests. The logging and manufacturing processes are expected to conform to the environmental regulations of the country of origin.

Impression number   10 9 8 7 6 5 4 3 2 1
Year   2009 2008 2007 2006 2005 2004

contents

introduction

Definitions

This book is specifically about special forces and will deal with their history, development, training, and their role in the war against terrorism. However, before we can begin learning about such elite units, we must first set down precisely what we mean by 'special forces'. This book will concern itself with small, specially recruited and trained bodies, either from the armed forces or law enforcement agencies, whose mission is to perform special tasks such as conducting raids in enemy territory, hostage rescues, siege busting and, in some cases, intelligence gathering as required by departments of national governments. In other words, engaging in the dirty work that is sometimes necessary in this dangerous age.

Thus, commando-type units are not included, such as the French Foreign Legion, US Rangers and Armoured Cavalry units, Royal Marine Commandos and any other larger unit that is at times called on to perform special missions. All too often, media reports may state that in Afghanistan or Iraq, 'US Special Forces were involved in a mission against suspected terrorists', without specifying what type of unit or how many men were involved. A case in point was the surrounding of Saddam Hussein's two sons in a house in Baghdad (22

July, 2003). Yes, unspecified special forces were employed, but so were tanks, infantry and jet aircraft. At the least, an infantry battalion was tasked, a gun battle lasting several hours ensued, and the media trumpeted the successful conclusion of the attack when the dead bodies had been carted out of the demolished house. That, however, went against the principles of a special forces' operation and was an application of overkill in relation to the object to be attained – the elimination of a few men with huge prices on their heads, holed up in a house. There were no hostages to be rescued and, if the objective was the termination of the two sons, one laser-guided bomb would have done the trick. Even better, an assault by a small elite unit using the classic parameters of speed, stealth and aggression.

Secrecy versus publicity

Special forces units, by their very nature, do not court publicity and their methods of operation tend to be kept as a closely guarded secret. In these dangerous times, countries who have a special forces capability tend to keep their units strictly under wraps for obvious reasons – their modus operandi should not be revealed to potential enemies in advance, and so it is difficult for any author to compile a comprehensive review of special forces worldwide. Thus, this book will concentrate upon the British Special Air Service Regiment (SAS), which started the fashion for such units and has become by far and away the best known for reasons which will be explained.

Special forces operating under a cloud of secrecy always excite public curiosity, and the media will do their best to satisfy this. I have a fat file of press cuttings, the majority of which can simply be dismissed as pure fantasy.

There was a prominent article recently in a British Sunday newspaper under a headline 'Like a rat in a trap' giving details of how Osama Bin Laden had been cornered by the SAS who were just waiting to spring the trap. However, I do not imagine that the US would permit their public enemy number one to be taken by the British! This is typical of the misinformation fed to the press where secret services are concerned.

The very first time the SAS received unwelcome publicity was in April 1980, when they stormed the Iranian embassy in the centre of London, England, which had been taken over by dissidents who had captured a number of hostages. When the terrorists started killing the hostages, the government had no choice but to call on the SAS who stormed the building under the eyes of journalists and TV cameras. We saw the men in black swarming down from the roof, blowing in the windows and disappearing inside. In a few minutes it was all over, the hostages bundled outside and the hostage takers, bar one, dead. This operation will be described in detail in Chapter 4, but the point is that people had been killed in broad daylight in a central London street and a formal inquest had to be held before a coroner. The soldiers involved had to appear identified only by letters, for example, 'Soldier I'.

The resulting publicity was unwelcome to the Regiment but it did lead to a huge boost in would-be recruits coming forward, requests for training assistance from around the world, and undoubtedly the deterrent effect was reinforced. After all, what is the point of an anti-terrorist unit if one does not demonstrate what it can do to deter future enemies?

Until the Iranian embassy operation, the SAS had operated in the shadows, and strenuous efforts were made to black out the faces and protect the identities of the men involved. The media was happy to co-operate with this. However, during the First Gulf War (1991), the SAS was in action in the Iraqi desert. Sir Peter de la Billière, the deputy commander of coalition forces, himself a highly decorated SAS soldier, saw fit to publish his memoirs in which he gave details of the patrol known as Bravo Two Zero; this was quite sensational. On the basis of what is good for senior officers is equally good for humble soldiers, the patrol commander, Andy McNab, published his own account of the operation which became a world best-seller and was made into a film. The floodgates were unleashed and, during the 1990s, a pile of memoirs and accounts was published, some of which were highly fanciful but gave an insight into the secret world of covert operations.

In this book, where proper names are used, they are already in the public domain but may well be pseudonyms. The authorities have now placed a gag on all members of the special forces in Britain. Those who have already published have been banished from the base, on the principle of bolting the stable door after the horse has escaped. One can counter that argument by making the point that members of special forces units are public servants, and the public is entitled to know about them providing that national security is not endangered – however that may be defined.

Police as opposed to military units

Most people are familiar with the statement that one person's terrorist is another person's freedom-fighter, co-religionist, patriot or whatever. The majority of European countries that have an anti-terror unit have preferred to confine that work to specially trained paramilitary police units, yet Britain has opted to use soldiers. The difference is that soldiers are trained and motivated to kill their enemies, whereas police officers are there to administer the law and arrest the wrongdoers. One of the major criticisms often levelled at the SAS is their excessive use of violence and that they are trained government thugs who can go around killing people at will. In modern times it is not exactly fashionable to kill one's enemies; society in general wants a nice 'clean' war without casualties, using precision-guided bombs which should not kill civilians or cause collateral damage. As recent conflicts have demonstrated, this is an impossibility. Often society is outraged by pictures of wounded civilians on the television, yet war is an unpleasant business and has been throughout history. It has long been an SAS principle to use the minimum force required to achieve the desired result.

The use of police officers against an enemy that all too often courts martyrdom is in itself illogical. The honest cop who pulls out a pair of handcuffs and says, 'OK, the game is up. Come on out with your hands up' is likely to get themselves shot. The modern terrorist is not your average petty criminal who may well decide to surrender rather than subject themselves to violence. The use of the SAS in Northern Ireland often led to controversy, and to them being called 'Maggie's killers', referring to Margaret Thatcher the then British Prime Minister who authorized many of the SAS operations against the IRA. Yet if you are dealing with a ruthless enemy, they have to be dealt with in a ruthless way. SAS troops in Northern Ireland were so often hampered by the rules of engagement which regulated the waging of war in a part of the United Kingdom and in the midst of a largely innocent population. Public opinion often became split along traditional political lines between 'right' and 'left'. Those on the right tended to rejoice when they read of a successful SAS operation resulting in the death of terrorists, whereas the left-wing liberal-thinking people were uneasy when, for example, the SAS shot dead three known IRA operatives in cold blood in a street in Gibraltar in front of numerous witnesses (see Chapter 4). The three victims became martyrs to their cause, assassinated in an extra judicial execution by their British oppressors. Here, one enters into a moral maze for which, often, there is no right answer. This book discusses the question of force necessary to combat the threat of terrorism. Should one use a highly trained group of soldiers, who are nevertheless answerable in law for their actions, or is it preferable to entrust the task to a police unit?

The SAS

In this book, considerable emphasis is placed on the history and activities of the British Special Air Service Regiment. For this, no apologies are made. The intention is not to belittle the operations of other special forces, but the SAS, under its founder David Stirling who invented the concept of raiding forces in the first place, was copied by others, and the SAS was the first to explore thoroughly the problems of counter-terrorist warfare. In addition, the SAS's history is far more fully documented.

Whether we like it or not, we are all caught up in the war against terrorism and the finest special forces could not have averted the 11 September 2001 attacks in the USA, unless specific evidence had been forthcoming and the perpetrators could have been apprehended. The fact that it was not is now the subject of countless investigations. Special forces are blind without precise intelligence.

01

special forces in the Second World War

This chapter will cover:
- how Britain's situation favoured the employment of special forces and unconventional warfare
- how resistance movements helped win the war for the Allies
- Churchill's order to 'set Europe ablaze' and the Special Operations Executive
- how David Stirling dreamed up the principles on which the SAS was based.

The concept of raiding is nothing new, and throughout the ages small groups have banded together to pull off daring feats – usually against their neighbours' property as well as during warfare. After all, Sir Francis Drake 'singed the King of Spain's beard', when he boldly sailed his ships into Cadiz harbour and cut out the ships being assembled to land an invading army in England during the reign of Elizabeth I. Perhaps the first to employ unconventional means of warfare was a certain Joshua, who used a brass band to breach the walls of Jericho, and the Greeks with their great ruse of the Trojan Horse in antiquity. For centuries cattle raiding was a national sport among the gentry, especially in Scotland, and the Americans invented a new word for it – rustling. Robin Hood was a byword for daring, if unconventional, exploits against the Sheriff of Nottingham. Historically, it has always been weaker nations (in terms of manpower) who have resorted to unconventional methods of warfare, and we get the words 'guerrilla' from Spain and 'commando' from South Africa. If the only way you can inflict serious damage on a large, well-armed enemy is by attacking supply lines and isolated bodies of troops, you may eventually win. The Viet Cong in Vietnam did just this by making the 1964–75 conflict too costly for the USA to bear. This is the tactic being employed by the modern Islamic terrorists.

The birth of special forces in Britain

Britain, a relatively small nation with a long history of unconventional warfare and individual daring, built a great empire on the basis of maritime power. Ships' captains, often working outside the laws governing piracy, helped to create the empire. During the Second World War, much of the credit for fostering the development of special forces must be given to Winston

Churchill, the then British Prime Minister, himself an unconventional warrior in many respects. Winston always had an open ear for anyone who devised methods, however crackbrained they were, to inflict damage on the enemy. When, in 1940, Britain stood alone against the might of Nazi Germany, Churchill issued his famous call to 'set Europe ablaze', which in turn led to the formation of the Special Operations Executive (SOE) with a mission to foment and support resistance movements. Various governments in exile established a presence in London and became a focus for their citizens who wished to continue the fight against Germany, and the SOE set up several country sections.

When France was occupied by the Germans in the summer of 1940, Britain was left alone to face up to Hitler, and many people advised making peace. However, the Prime Minister had no intention of caving in. Britain had no armies left to send to France and no prospect of bringing battle to the European continent, and thus had to consider resorting to irregular warfare. But, how to set about it?

Auxiliary Units

Threatened by the very real prospect of immediate invasion, Churchill authorized the establishment of the Auxiliary Units, the first special forces initiative in Britain. Long shrouded in total secrecy, these units were stay-behind parties designed to go to ground if the Germans invaded. Recruited by word of mouth, largely from country dwellers, the units received some training, were expected to select their own hides and then sally forth to raid the enemy's rear areas. Never actually used, the Auxiliary Units continued in training until the threat of invasion passed, and became a useful source of recruits for the SAS in 1944.

Commandos

Although, strictly speaking, Commandos are beyond the scope of this book, they must be mentioned at this stage because they were used for raiding purposes, and many special forces personalities emerged from their ranks or were trained by them. Originally known as Independent Companies, several units were raised during the spring of 1941 and first saw service after the German invasion of Norway. The Independent Companies were absorbed into the Commando units later on in the same year. Recruiting from volunteers, the Commandos tended to absorb the adventurous spirits who were bored by the pettiness of military regulations in orthodox units and were eager to fight the enemy. There was some criticism that the Commandos tended to cream off the best men from a unit, but gradually a total of 11 Commando units was raised, organized later on into the Special Service Battalions. They were not generally airborne trained, but Commandos developed a strong maritime specialty, coming ashore from landing craft that had to be designed to carry them. While the bulk of Britain's armed forces sat along the coast ready to ward off invasion, and the fighter pilots of the Royal Air Force (RAF) did battle with the *Luftwaffe*, the Commandos were the first to raid the enemy shores, thus helping to lift the nation's morale.

The origins of the SAS

Early in 1941, three Commando units, numbers 7, 8 and 11, sailed for the Middle East under the command of Colonel Bob Laycosk, taking its name, Layforce, from him. One of the men was a subaltern in the Scots Guards, a second lieutenant by the name of David Stirling. Immensely tall, Stirling came from an ancient Scottish aristocratic family, the Stirlings of Keir. On leaving school he had gone to Paris to study painting, but soon discovered that he lacked talent, whereupon he decided to climb Mount Everest. As part of his training for this challenge, Stirling undertook several climbs in the Rockies, where the outbreak of war caught up with him. He hurried back to Scotland and was commissioned into the Scots Guards, where he found life at the depot to be dull. One of the early volunteers for the Commandos, Stirling found the outdoor training, with his background as a sportsman, far more to his taste and he was sent to learn skiing in the French Alps when the Germans invaded France.

On arrival in Egypt, only part of Layforce was employed, fighting the Vichy French in the Lebanon and Syria, and Stirling found himself with nothing much to do apart from enjoying the fleshpots of wartime Cairo. Fate, however, took a hand when a fellow officer, Jock Lewes, discovered some parachutes, and he and Stirling obtained permission from Laycock to experiment with them. Together with a few guardsmen, the two officers, without any ground training whatsoever, managed to obtain the use of an aged biplane from the RAF and set off for their first jump. They tied their static lines around the legs of the aircraft seats, but Stirling's parachute became snagged around the tail of the plane, which tipped out two panels, causing him to make a heavy landing. That episode landed him in hospital for two months with two paralysed legs and bad back injuries.

Stirling's idea

He may have been immobilized, but Stirling's imagination roved far and wide over the desert war. German Lieutenant General Rommel had arrived on the scene, and Britain was hard-pressed to defend Egypt and the Suez Canal. Scribbling his ideas down on sheets of paper, Stirling argued that Rommel's supply lines, strung along the coast, were extremely vulnerable, but that raids by the Commandos were far too unwieldy and the British navy could not spare ships to transport the men. What was needed was a raiding force that was economic on manpower and equipment. Stirling proposed a basic sub-unit of five men, later reduced to four, transportable by air, sea or land, able to carry out raids against multiple targets during one night. The unit should be directly responsible to the commander-in-chief and not be subjected to any other formation, and that those carrying out such raids should also plan them. Stirling's first mission proposed to raid the enemy's forward airfields and destroy the aircraft on the ground, going in by parachute and being brought out by the vehicles of the Long Range Desert Group (LRDG).

Having outlined his idea, Stirling was confronted with the difficulty of how to deliver it into the hands of the commander-in-chief of the Middle East, General Auchinleck. Once he had prepared the proposal during June and July 1941, Stirling got out of the hospital and was driven to the Middle East Headquarters (MEHQ). There he failed to get past the sentry, but hobbled through a gap in the wire. Once inside, he stumbled into the office of General Ritchie, deputy chief of staff, who instead of throwing the intruder out, read through the paper and promised to hand it personally to the commander-in-chief. The upshot was that Stirling was promoted to captain and authorized to recruit a total of 60 men and six officers from the remnants of Layforce, and was given an area of land beside the Suez Canal as a base. His new unit was to be called L Detachment Special Air Service Brigade. There was no such air brigade but the aim was to convince the Germans and Italians that Britain had an airborne force in the Middle East.

The Long Range Desert Group

This group needs a short introduction at this stage because its history is intertwined with that of the SAS in the early period of operations in the Middle East. Before the war, a small group of enthusiasts, both British and French, had pioneered long-distance desert travel. One of these enthusiasts, Major Bagnold, formed the LRDG strictly as a reconnaissance unit to gather intelligence behind enemy lines. Making use of the empty desert, patrols covered vast distances in Chevrolet trucks to gather information of any movements, but were not tasked to carry out offensive operations.

The formation of the SAS

Still injured, Captain David Stirling travelled through the camps housing the Commandos of Layforce looking for likely volunteers. He looked for individualists who had self-discipline. He wanted tough men whose toughness was reserved for the enemy: bar-room brawlers were not tolerated. Having collected his first 60 men, these men were told that their first operation would be to steal their own camp. This they did after dark by raiding the camp of the New Zealand Division who were away fighting at the front. They even stole a piano for the officers' mess.

Jock Lewes was placed in charge of training, and proved highly effective. There was no parachute school in the Middle East, so an instructor was sent out from England and jumping towers were built from scaffold poles. Lewes had rowed for Oxford and had seen action, raiding enemy outposts in Tobruk. Another of the officers was Blair 'Paddy' Mayne, a giant of a man and an international rugby player for Ireland. The training programme was rigorous; anyone not up to standard was simply seeded out and returned to their parent unit (RTU'd). Stirling insisted on high standards of smartness and discipline from his men at all times, but he did not impose petty restrictions. Minor disputes were settled by the sergeant-major's fists in the boxing ring.

Constantly hindered by the obstructive attitude of staff officers, Stirling had to use all his powers of tact and diplomacy to get his unit supplied with everything they needed. Within three months they were declared ready to operate.

With training finished the men of L Detachment Special Air Service Brigade, who later became known as 'The Originals', were fused together as a credible fighting force with intense pride in themselves and their unit. At this stage they adopted the famous winged dagger badge and the SAS parachute wings as well as their motto, 'Who Dares, Wins'. Besides his role as trainer, Jock Lewes had also invented the Lewes Bomb, capable of blowing a hole through an aircraft wing and setting the petrol tanks alight. Weighing only one pound, each man could carry 20.

The first operation

This operation was in support of General Auchinleck's offensive, code-named 'Crusader', designed to push Rommel back and secure advance airfields from which the convoys to Malta could be protected. It was planned to commence on 17 November 1941. L Detachment Special Air Service Brigade was to drop the night before, close to their targets and just before the main attack, slip down to the coastal plain, place their bombs on the parked aircraft and slip away to a desert rendezvous where they would be picked up by an LRGD patrol.

The men's morale was high as they arrived at an advanced landing strip where five Bristol Bombay aircraft were waiting for them – ancient under-powered transport machines that had been converted for parachuting. There the men found out that a gale was brewing but decided to go ahead with the operation anyway. The aircraft staggered through the night and the drop was carried out, but several injuries were sustained as the men were dragged across the desert by their parachutes. Added to this, several containers containing vital equipment were missing. In fact, two of the five paratrooper groups went missing and only four officers and 18 other ranks survived to fight another day. The operation was a total disaster but the necessary lessons were learned the hard way. The major offensive also stalled and thankfully nobody had time to bother with what L Detachment was up to.

Further steps

Stirling realized that if the LRDG could pick up his men, in future they could also drive them closer to their targets as parachuting in those early days was a far too unreliable method of insertion. He gathered his depleted force at Jalo Oasis where there was a motorized column on the southern flank of the main army. Stirling was determined not to show that he had been beaten and, ever the optimist, he planned a series of raids on enemy airfields along the coast, splitting into four groups. Three raids were planned for the night of 14 December and piled on top of the LRDG trucks, the raiders set off with high hopes. Stirling himself had no luck as his party was spotted by a sentry who raised the alarm. However, as they were retreating to the rendezvous, they spotted flashes in the distance, demonstrating that Mayne's group had found their prey. When Mayne came into the

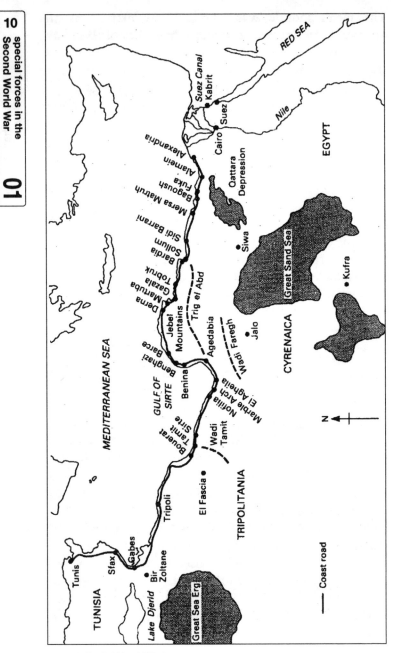

figure 1 North Africa 1941–3

meeting point he said that he had destroyed 28 enemy aircraft as well as stocks of petrol until they had run out of bombs.

And so they continued, carrying out further raids on airfields a few days later, but these were marred by a sad loss. The patrol carrying Jock Lewes's party was returning to Jalo when it was spotted by an enemy aircraft and strafed, killing Lewes. This became the pattern for raids during the early months of 1942 as the tiny group with no time to train-up replacements, carried on their campaign of destruction. Aircraft, vehicles, stores etc. were all used to advantage and Stirling could return to base to find more recruits and plan his further moves.

General Auchinleck had heard of the successes of L Detachment Special Air Service Brigade and was pleased, giving the commander a cordial reception. Stirling, who had a good sense of strategy, realized that Rommel was retreating, and reckoned that his supply lines would be highly vulnerable. Therefore he proposed to attack the small port of Bouerat in the Gulf of Sirte to destroy any shipping found.

Stirling, who was promoted to major, also received permission to recruit 40 more men and several officers. For the last series of raids, both he and Paddy Mayne were awarded the DSO. For the next raid Stirling decided to leave Paddy back at base in order to supervize training, including the training of a group of Free French soldiers, already parachute trained and a welcome reinforcement.

The Special Boat Section (SBS)

The SBS emerged from the Commandos. A certain Roger Courtney, who had joined the Commandos with David

Stirling, had started training in the Scottish lochs with folboats, German designed folding canoes. Courtney and his group had come out to the Middle East with Layforce and had been carrying out raids on the Italian coast. Stirling managed to get two of them attached for the raid on Bouerat, which left for Jalo Oasis in early January 1942. The SBS detachment came equipped with limpet mines to attach to any ships found.

The desert patrols slipped into a routine, with the SAS men sitting on top of the heavily laden LRDG trucks, weighed down with food, water, spares and plenty of ammunition. They drove by day, often hundreds of miles inside enemy territory – and detailed maps of the desert were non-existent. One constant worry was being observed from the air and another was becoming bogged down in patches of sand forcing everyone to dismount in order to extricate the vehicle. Navigation was by means of a sextant to fix the position. Laying up to sleep, the trucks were covered with camouflage netting if there was no natural cover available. The conditions were extreme – blistering heat during the day and freezing cold temperatures at night. When in the desert, many of the men wore Arab headdress and sported beards.

The raiding force got into Bouerat without injury, other than to the SBS canoe, which was wrecked. Finding there were no guards, the men slipped into the harbour area but found no ships in port. Instead, the SBS men dealt with the harbour radio station while the SAS placed their bombs in the warehouses and on several large petrol tankers. All men returned safely to base only to discover that Jalo was being abandoned as Rommel had counter-attacked and thrown the Eighth Army back to the Egyptian frontier.

Stirling's next plan was for a series of raids around Benghazi, some 640 kilometres (400 miles) west along the coast. Stirling's group went off from Siwa and made their way to the coast road, driving into the port without any problems. There they managed a thorough recce but did not place any bombs so as not to alert the enemy – the intention was to return one day. In an example of bare-faced cheek, as they were leaving the port area, Fitzroy Maclean, a recent officer recruit, had the guard turned out and gave them a dressing down for their slovenly appearance. The entire party made their way back to Siwa somewhat disappointed.

In the Spring of 1942, the Eighth Army was holding the Gazala Line and General Auchinleck was being urged by Churchill to attack in order to relieve the pressure on Malta. As far as the SAS was concerned, Stirling was struggling to stop his unit from being absorbed into some larger formation and also to bring it back up to strength. Various commanding officers were resisting Stirling's efforts to poach their best men, but he did manage to absorb a unit known as the Special Interrogation Group, which consisted of Germans, mostly Jews, who had volunteered to fight for the Allied cause. In early June he was planning a return to the airfields around Benghazi as well as a descent on Crete, using the Free French who were, by then, operational.

However, whilst Stirling's group headed off along the coast they heard that Tobruk had fallen and that the Eighth Army had suffered a major defeat. The Eighth Army had been hurled back to the El Alamein Line, the last defence before the Nile, where it was expected that the Germans would shortly arrive. Stirling's raids were successful in destroying aircraft and transport and those involved had experience of being behind the enemy lines. They travelled to Crete by submarine and carried out another successful raid, destroying over 20 aircraft in the Heraklion airfield. While the raiders returned to Siwa, Stirling headed to Cairo where he found the headquarters in a panic and documents being burned. The first week in July 1942 marked an abrupt change in the SAS mode of operation. L Detachment Special Air Services Brigade by then numbered about 100 men, mostly trained, and if the Germans broke through, plans were being made to escape south into the desert in order to continue raiding.

Stirling realized the importance of having their own transport and managed to lay his hands on some newly arrived jeeps, as well as a stock of twin Vickers aircraft machine guns. As the men struggled to equip the jeeps, they evolved into what must be the most cost-effective fighting vehicles of all time.

The SAS jeep had a water condenser fitted in front of the radiator grille and an extra fuel tank. In terms of firepower it was normally equipped with twin Vickers to the front and rear, although on some versions, the front Vickers were replaced by a Browning .5 calibre heavy machine gun. Magazines were loaded with a mixture of explosive, tracer and incendiary rounds that proved lethal when used against aircraft and road transport targets. The jeeps normally carried a crew of three and were festooned with jerrycans of petrol, water containers, spare pancake magazines, camouflage netting, sand channels as well as the crew's personal kit and weapons.

Raiding continued as before on the German and Italian forward airfields and the jeeps proved to be highly successful, but they were limited as to the amount of time they could spend in the desert as supplies had to be carried. At that time there were no facilities for air drops and men had to constantly drive back to Kabrit to fetch replacement vehicles, food and water for the operational area.

In a series of raids later that month, Stirling developed a new method of operation by deciding to drive onto an airfield. In a famous raid on Sidi Hemeish airfield, he set out with 18 jeeps on the night of 20 July 1942. The vehicles were split into two columns which were to crash their way through the perimeter and drive down the runway shooting everything they saw. Like a Nelsonian fleet of battleships firing broadsides, the two columns sped down the runway, the scene illuminated by blazing aircraft. The SAS claimed that a total of 40 aircraft were destroyed, for the loss of one man killed and two jeeps wrecked.

At the end of July, L Detachment Special Air Services Brigade was ordered back to base and Stirling was summoned to Cairo. Also at that time, Winston Churchill came out to the Middle East and determined on a change of command. Auchinleck departed for India, to be replaced by General Alexander. Montgomery was appointed to command the Eighth Army. Montgomery fought and won the preliminary Battle of Alam Halfa in early September 1943 and was planning his knock-out blow against Rommel for November.

The L Detachment Special Air Service Brigade's freebooting days under independent command were now over; they were henceforth to come under a staff command known as Raiding Force. However, the SAS was granted regimental status and Stirling was promoted to colonel. Expanded to a total of four squadrons and a headquarters, there were new recruits to be trained and raids to be made all along the coast on Rommel's supply lines. Stirling was forbidden to take part owing to his knowledge of Allied plans. Mayne took most of the original L Detachment Special Air Service Brigade men and formed A Squadron, which kept up the pressure on Rommel by raiding his supply lines and the coastal railway. Victory at El Alamein was followed by the Anglo-American Torch landings in Algeria in early November, which trapped Rommel between the two Allied armies.

B Squadron consisted of the new boys. One of them, David Sutherland, was sent up into Austria with the SBS men to train for offensive water-borne operations in the Mediterranean. The SBS had been reinforced by a group of Greeks known as the Sacred Squadron. At the other end of the combat zone, Sriekig's brother Bill was raising a second SAS regiment in Algeria. It was at this transitional stage that David Stirling set off on his last trip into the desert.

Stirling's capture

The new members of B Squadron had an uneventful journey west into what was new territory for the SAS. By then enemy supplies were being routed through the Tunisian port of Gabes, where the coastal plain narrowed to form a gap. On this last desert patrol, B Squadron had little luck and most of the inexperienced crews ended up either being killed or captured, as they got tangled up with the retreating Germans. Stirling, along with five other jeeps, decided to drive through the Gabes gap, following Jordan and his Free French patrol some 12 hours ahead of them. However, the latter had had a shoot out with some Germans and thereby alerted the enemy. Stirling's group drove serenely along the coast road all mixed up with enemy vehicles in broad daylight. It seems quite astonishing that the desert stained jeeps, laden with kit and crewed by ruffianly looking unshaven men could do this, but that was what the SAS was all about.

On the morning of 24 January 1943, they drove through a German armoured column and then decided to stop for a rest. They drove off the road into a wadi (valley), covered with scrub bushes and the men dispersed to get what sleep they could. After the long drive they were understandably tired, yet for some reason Stirling failed to post sentries and soon Germans began to comb the wadi. Stirling himself was trapped in a cave but three of the men managed to get away in the confusion. Thus ended the career of the man the Germans called the 'Phantom Major'. He spent the rest of the war as a prisoner, making several attempts to escape and finally ended up in Colditz.

Sicily and Italy

Re-organization

The loss of David Stirling and his invaluable sense of diplomacy was keenly felt by his friends in high places. By the end of January 1943 British Special Forces were widely dispersed. Paddy Mayne was up in Lebanon learning to ski with the men of A Squadron. Lord Jellicoe had been left in charge of training at Kabrit and the survivors of B Squadron were still coming back from the desert. Sutherland was in Palestine with the bulk of the SBS and the French Squadron, with some of the Greeks, was raiding in Tunisia. It is very difficult to track the movements of Special Forces in the early part of 1943 as there is almost a total lack of official documents available.

What emerges is that Paddy Mayne was given command of the remaining members of 1 SAS Regiment, which was reduced to a single squadron and became known as the Special Raiding Squadron (SRS), numbering approximately 250 men, and divided into three large troops. Jellicoe took over the SBS, which henceforth had its own separate identity, although it retained SAS insignia. The French and Greeks reverted to their own national commands and Bill Stirling's 2 SAS Regiment remained in Algeria.

Once Tunisia had been finally cleared of the remains of the *Afrika Korps*, the Allies planned to invade Sicily, the soft underbelly of Europe – it was intended that both the SRS and 2 SAS would be involved. What is clear is that

Sicily and Italy 1943–4

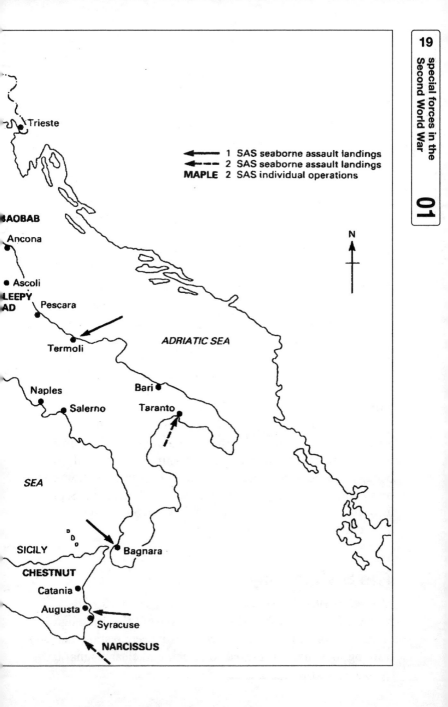

1 SAS seaborne assault landings
2 SAS seaborne assault landings
MAPLE 2 SAS individual operations

Trieste

N

BAOBAB
Ancona

Ascoli
SLEEPY AD
Pescara

Termoli

ADRIATIC SEA

Naples
Salerno

Bari
Taranto

SEA

SICILY
CHESTNUT
Catania
Augusta
Syracuse
NARCISSUS

Bagnara

they were to be used en masse as shock infantry rather then as small raiding parties, thus diluting David Stirling's original principles. The SRS became, in fact, a commando unit that was far too unwieldy in Stirling's eyes for covert operations. However, it has to be said that they were going to operate in a densely populated country without the wide open desert to disappear into.

The base at Kabrit was abandoned and the SRS was assembled in Palestine to train for operations that, once again, included the use of landing craft. The two squadrons were welded into one by Mayne, mixing in the 'originals' with the newcomers and they had to learn to fight together. The invasion of Sicily was known as Operation Husky and it was planned that the SRS would attack a heavy gun battery overlooking the port of Syracuse, as the vanguard of the invasion force. The fleet sailed from Suez in early July and arrived off the Sicilian coast in a rough sea that made it difficult to launch the landing craft from the larger ship carrying the unit. They managed, however, to get ashore without incident, scrambling up the cliffs and neutralizing the battery. They then cleared another battery, demolished the guns and managed to amass several hundred not unwilling prisoners, all for the loss of one man. The unit was re-embarked on the mother ship and set sail to occupy the port of Augusta where it encountered some opposition. Mayne proved that he could lead the SAS into battle and, for the brief foray in Sicily, he was awarded a bar to his DSO.

The SRS in Italy

Montgomery led his Eighth Army across the Straits of Messina on 3 September 1943, at the start of the campaign on the mainland. The SRS, who had been resting and training in Sicily, was tasked to attack and clear Bagnara, just to the north of the main landing area. However, here intervened a classic case of Special Forces not being responsible for their own transport. The fault lay with the navy and inexperienced landing craft skippers who managed to run aground before they hit the beach and then wanted to turn back. Their passengers had to use force to persuade the skippers to run in and put them ashore. The men ended up on the wrong side of the bay but were welcomed as liberators by the townspeople. Soon, however, German mortars on the surrounding hills opened up – the SRS held on to the place for three days until regular troops arrived to relieve them.

After that the SRS returned once again to Sicily where they camped until required for their last mission in Italy – the Battle of Termoli – that was to cost them dearly in terms of casualties. Termoli was a harbour town north of Bari where the Eighth Army was trying to break through. It was decided that the Special Service Brigade was to be sent in to capture the port. The Brigade consisted of a number of Allied Commandos and their job was to facilitate the advance of a division coming up from the south. On 3 October 1943, the 200 men of the SRS arrived at the port in a large landing craft and when the Commandos had secured the beach they were signaled in, but promptly ran aground. They had to transfer themselves and their equipment into smaller craft in order to be ferried ashore, where they passed through the Commando's perimeter and achieved their objectives against serious opposition.

By midday they were pulled back into the town as regular troops arrived and assumed that the battle was over and done with. There they met up with a small party from 2 SAS, the first time they had been together on a battlefield. There followed a couple of quiet days but the indications were that the enemy was planning a counter-attack. Mayne was playing billiards with some of his officers when shells started exploding. He remarked that they should finish the game and then go and see what was happening! Under attack by paratroopers it was a question of plugging the gaps in the lines. One section piled into a captured truck as a shell burst on the men in the back. The battle raged on into the night but the situation was stabilized the following morning with the arrival of Canadian tanks and a brigade of infantry in the harbour.

Termoli ended the campaign in Italy as far as the SRS was concerned and they were pulled back to Bari where boredom set in. They had been totally misused in the Italian campaign and nobody seemed to know what to do with them. However, in December, Paddy Mayne was ordered to proceed to Scotland with an advance party to plan their move home where they were to prepare for operations in France.

2 SAS in Sicily and Italy

Bill Stirling, like his brother, had started off in the Scots Guards and then transferred to the Commandos. There he drifted into the Small Scale Raiding Force, also known as No. 62 Commando. The unit was used for cross-Channel raiding but went to Algeria with the Torch landings in November 1942, where nobody knew what to do with it. Bill obtained permission from Allied Forces HQ to raise a second SAS regiment, on exactly the same principles as 1 SAS and was given a camp on the coast at Phillipeville. He managed to recruit a number of experienced men from his own disbanded 62 Commando unit but had to train his recruits from scratch. Also in the area was Lord Jellicoe with an SBS detachment.

The earliest operations were small raids on the Mediterranean islands of Lampedusa and Pantellaria, and later Sardinia – these were combined SAS/SBS affairs. Unlike his brother David, Bill preferred to leave raiding to his squadron commanders and was better employed at headquarters organizing his regiment. This regiment was to be involved in the Sicily landing in two ways. First, a landing party to capture a lighthouse and, second, the dropping of some small parachute parties to disrupt enemy communications in the north of the island. The latter was far more in keeping with what the SAS was good at, but the missions achieved very little. However, it is worth noting that 2 SAS were far better employed in Italy in small parties than was the case for the SRS.

2 SAS was divided into four British squadrons, little more than troops in size, plus a French squadron consisting mainly of ex-Legionaries. After the landings in Italy, the bulk of the regiment embarked on a mission to capture the port of Taranto, but in the meanwhile Italy had surrendered so the landing was unopposed. Italy may have become a friendly territory, but the country remained infested with Germans still determined to put up a fight. Operation Speedwell was more in true SAS style – it entailed dropping a number of small parties into northern Italy to sabotage the main railway lines. However, little thought had been given to how the men would be recovered. The result was a successful series of demolitions, and several epic foot marches the length of the country to regain Allied lines. Quite a number of the parachutists were unfortunately captured and some were never heard of again.

In the previous section much was made of the meeting at Termoli with the SRS. The reason that 2 SAS were there was to set up a base for small parties to land along the Adriatic coast to bring off freed Allied prisoners who were roaming the countryside as their guards had simply disappeared. Quite a number of prisoners were rounded up but few were brought off the Adriatic coast owing to boats failing to keep their rendezvous with the shore parties. There were a number of other minor raids but when winter set in the regiment was withdrawn to North Africa where they busied themselves with making good their losses with replacements who had to be trained. In April, they embarked on Scotland where they were to join 1 SAS, once again a regiment for further combat in north west Europe.

the new world tensions

This chapter will cover:
- what happened to the SAS and its offshoots in 1945
- how the Office of Strategic Services (OSS) became absorbed into the embryo CIA.

The post-war situation in Europe

Second World War hostilities ceased with the signing of the unconditional surrender of Germany on 9 May 1945. Germany was dismembered and divided up into zones of occupation – US, Soviet, British, and a zone as consolation for the French. Throughout the war-weary nations, the military bureaucrats and traditional thinkers heaved a sigh of relief that they could get back to some 'proper soldiering'. By that they meant the rapid disbandment of the various private armies that had sprung up to wage unconventional warfare

On both the eastern and western sides of the European divide, various agencies swarmed over the carcass of Nazi Germany to gather up what they could in the way of scientists and new weaponry. Otherwise, the various victorious armies settled down to administering their occupation zones but it soon became apparent that four-power control was a myth, and two of the sides increasingly went their own ways, separated by the Iron Curtain in what was to become known as the 'Cold War'.

The fate of the SAS

The war had left Britain financially ruined but still clinging to its imperial tradition. When hostilities ended, the two British SAS Regiments were immediately pulled out of Germany and dispatched to Norway where they had the task of disarming and repatriating the considerable German garrison in place there. Not facing any opposition, they could treat their stay in a friendly country as a holiday and a reward for their labours in combat. The unwieldy German brigade had already started to be broken up when the two French Regiments and the Belgian squadron were handed back to their respective armies, and it is interesting to note that even today, one of the French parachute regiments still wears the winged dagger badge of the SAS derived from its wartime assignment.

While the SAS was mopping up in Norway, the decision was made to disband it and simply discharge personnel back from whence they had come. On 5 October 1945 the final parades were held and the SAS ceased to exist, except for skeleton staffs handing back stores and processing the men leaving for civilian life. There was no army of counsellors to ease that abrupt transition – they had not been invented in those distant days – and those elite soldiers were simply left to get on with their lives as best they could. In fact, most of them were able to build up successful civilian careers, but of those who stayed in the army, none of them reached high rank. As far as the army was concerned, it was as if they had never existed. Some soldiers turned to drink, one or two later rejoined the reborn SAS, while others were absorbed into the intelligence community or went abroad to seek their fortunes in the colonies, including David Stirling. When freed from Colditz, where he had been imprisoned after being captured by Germans in 1943, Stirling departed for Africa where he founded a society devoted to the concept of Africanization.

The SAS, however, did not entirely disappear. One group was sent to Greece to oversee the payment of claims by Greek nationals against the British government, and inevitably ended up becoming involved in the civil war there on the Royalist side against the communists. Another small group went off to Germany to hunt down and bring to justice those responsible for the execution of numerous SAS prisoners, mainly in France during the war. This was a strictly freelance effort initiated by Colonel Brian Franks who had commanded 2 SAS Regiment, quite a number of whom had been murdered by the Gestapo in Alsace in 1944. Franks sent his intelligence officer, Major Eric 'Bill' Barkworth with a small team, wearing SAS shoulder flashes and cap badges, to Europe to find those responsible. During three years of painstaking detective work, they moved around Europe arresting suspects and giving evidence at the subsequent trials for war crimes.

Behind the scenes, there were those who were determined that the principles on which the SAS was founded should not die with the passing of the Regiment, and an intense lobbying campaign was carried out, much of it by Brian Franks. He had returned to his old job of general manager of the Hyde Park Hotel, the bar which became an unofficial meeting place for the demobilized and bored.

Meanwhile, the War Office was interested in the future of SAS-type formations, and solicited the views of a number of senior officers who had been involved. They submitted a concise number of recommendations to the Directorate of Tactical Investigation, emphasizing the ways in which SAS-type formations had contributed to the final victory and how their skills were still needed. Eventually the lobbying paid off, and in 1947 the SAS was reborn as a Territorial Army (TA) unit based in London with the title of 21 SAS Regiment. Many of the wartime operatives flocked to join, and its first commanding officer was none other than Lieutenant Colonel Brian Franks who had done so much to keep the spirit alive.

Similar disbandment was in store for all the other clandestine warfare and raiding units that had sprung up in Britain during the war years. The Special Operations Executive (SOE) was dissolved with indecent haste, many of its operatives being recruited into various intelligence-gathering agencies and counter-intelligence work in Germany for the occupation authorities. In the latter situation, they had to gather information on attempts to foster communism by the Russians.

The Special Boat Section (SBS) became subsumed into the Royal Marines, initially at Eastney Barracks near Portsmouth in England in 1947. Its tradition continues today as a branch of the marines, who have also taken on the command units.

After the Second World War, Britain all too soon became involved in a local war against terrorism. Paradoxically, the terrorism involved Jews and Palestinians in Palestine, an area which was governed by Britain under a mandate. Jewish immigration from Europe to Palestine was encouraged by various Zionist organizations but discouraged by the British as they feared opposition from the Arab majority. It was in this conflict that the seeds of the twenty-first-century Middle East conflagration were sown. Various extreme Zionist terror groups were formed to fight the British, and started an all too familiar campaign of assassinations and bombings in Palestine against the police who had recruited several SAS professionals, notably Roy Farran. The main Jewish group was the Irgun, a member of which was their later Prime Minister, Menachim Begin. One of the most spectacular targets was the King David Hotel in Jerusalem which was blown up, killing several civilians.

The United States

The US had experienced less direct contact with occupied Europe, which to a large extent it had liberated at enormous cost and expense. It was, however, William 'Wild Bill' Donovan's Office of Strategic Services (OSS), whose agents had successfully taken part in the inter-allied Jedburgh missions into the occupied territories behind enemy lines. There they had gained experience of training partisans and local resistance forces, arming them and motivating then to fight the common enemy. They themselves had been trained in the SOE schools in all the latest methods of sabotage, silent killing and subversion, and were not disbanded after hostilities ended. Instead, they were absorbed into the fledgling CIA (Central Intelligence Agency), which became responsible for psychological warfare, raising guerrilla groups in occupied territories, and subversion. In the post-war era the agents found a ready field for their activities in eastern Europe and the Far East: the CIA recruited dissident groups and refugees to infiltrate, notably in the Baltic States, and to fight the Russian occupiers, without much success it has to be admitted. Regrettably, many of the recruits turned out to have unfortunate pasts as Nazi sympathizers and, in a Russian context, many of the 'terrorists' were ruthlessly eliminated by the KGB (*Komitet gosvdarstvennon bezopasnosti* – Committee of State Security). The Americans were soon to be embroiled in Vietnam which saw the birth of their own special forces tradition, whereas Britain became involved in a series of post-colonial conflicts and found the need to resurrect a new regular SAS regiment.

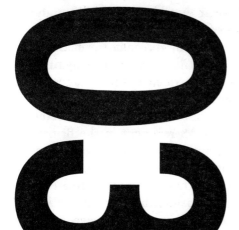

03

post-colonial conflicts

This chapter will cover:
- how the nature of conflict changed after the Second World War
- how the concept of special forces was reintroduced
- post-colonial conflicts in Malaya, Borneo and South Arabia and how they developed the fighting methods of special forces.

In the immediate post-war world, Britain naturally sought to regain control of her far-flung empire, as did France and the Netherlands. All three, however, were embroiled in savage guerrilla-style wars against insurgents fighting for independence. The so-called 'Malayan Emergency' was a classic case of Britain 'losing every battle except the last one', and was to lead directly to the formation of a new SAS regiment in the British army to reassert British authority over its extensive colonial empire throughout the world, much to the chagrin of the Americans. Yet times were changing and many colonies, having had a taste of life without British dominance during the Second World War, yearned for their independence. In addition, British prestige had suffered as its colonial subjects had witnessed the British army being booted out ignominiously by the Japanese from South-East Asia. After the surrender of Japan, Britain returned to the area, as did the Dutch, seemingly confident that life would continue as before. There had been a resistance movement in Malaya during the Japanese occupation, fomented and armed by SOE agents, and it was these guerrillas, retaining their arms supplied by Britain, who set out to turn them (the Malayans) against their erstwhile colonial masters. It was one of the planks of Soviet foreign policy to export the joys of communism to enrich those oppressed peoples in the colonies everywhere.

The French found themselves fighting to retain their hold on Indo-China, then Algeria. The USA took over where the French had left off in Indo-China/Vietnam; a war had to be fought to prevent a communist takeover of the entire Korean Peninsular. Britain found herself fighting insurgents in Malaya, then in southern Arabia, Borneo and Oman. Counter-insurgency warfare, by its guerrilla nature, in turn called for special countermeasures which often resulted in the discovery of the need for special forces, for instance, as the Cold War hotted up.

Britain, as the country with the most experience of special forces during the Second World War, had disbanded such specialist units with indecent haste and was singularly ill-placed to fight guerrilla wars in unfamiliar territory. In Korea, Britain sent conventional troops equipped to fight a conventional war, and America did the same. The general feeling was that there was no need for small-scale raiding forces in such a densely populated environment. However, there was one exception. Reportedly on the initiative of the US, Britain was requested to provide an SAS squadron. Major Greville-Bell, an experienced wartime officer, thus formed what was known as M Squadron SAS and it seems that recruitment was largely by word of mouth, partly from the TA regiment and partly from reservists.

It is unclear whether M Squadron ever got to fight in Korea; what is known is that the men were finally diverted to Singapore where they became B Squadron of the Malayan Scouts.

The Malayan emergency

This conflict started with an act of terrorism when three British rubber planters were murdered on their estates in June 1948 by Chinese communist terrorists who became known as CTs for short. Operating from camps hidden in the dense jungle, they preyed on the soft targets presented by the isolated plantations and mines throughout the country. Heavily laden regular troops, restricted to the few roads, were powerless to intervene to protect civilians. An early expedient was the formation of Ferret Force from civilian volunteers with wartime experience, which managed to eliminate some CT camps. However, they were too few in numbers, and the murders continued.

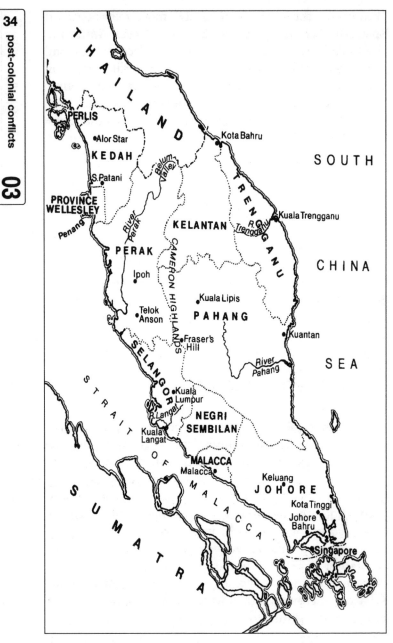

figure 3 Malaya during the emergency

The commander-in-chief in the Far East was General (later Field Marshal) Sir John Narding who, early in 1950, decided to seek some advice from 'Mad' Mike Calvert, who had been the final commander of the unwieldy SAS Brigade during the final stages of the Second World War. Mike Calvert was cooling his heels in Hong Kong, but was the ideal man as he had fought behind the lines in Burma and had experience of irregular warfare.

Calvert proposed the formation of special units able to patrol in the jungle for long periods, and who could befriend the aboriginal tribes to wean them away from supporting the insurgents. By denying them their food supplies, they would be forced out into the open where police and army units could mop them up. Calvert was given authority to recruit a force, initially of 100 men, which was called the Malayan Scouts (SAS). He trawled the Far East and collected a nucleus of Burma veterans who became A Squadron, but without a thorough selection process they soon gained an unsavoury reputation for indiscipline and excessive drinking. This rough, tough bunch was raised without any input from the SAS TA unit in England but did contain some excellent men.

Soon the Malayan Scouts received further reinforcements when a group of volunteers arrived who had been destined to fight in Korea and joined forces to become B Squadron. Its sergeant-major was Bob Bennet who had been one of David Stirling's 'originals' from the desert and who had fought right throughout the Second World War with the Regiment. C Squadron was also added, consisting of Rhodesian volunteers. In those early days in Malaya the SAS gained a reputation for being a cowboy outfit. In the autumn of 1951, Calvert invalided back to England suffering from extreme fatigue and was replaced by Cil Sloane, a regular officer who pulled the patrols out of the jungle and instituted a period or retraining, instilling basic military discipline.

Sloane's training proved very valuable. B Squadron had the only pool of trained parachutists and as there was no parachutist school in the Far East, improvisation was resorted to for the rest of the unit, which was slated to return to the jungle in February 1952. The first large-scale operation proved unsuccessful. A and C Squadrons approached the target area on foot while B Squadron parachuted in. However, the noise made by the foot parties was so excessive that every CT had time to decamp. The SAS soon learned the value of stealth in jungle operations.

The Regiment had had no previous experience of jungle fighting, and thus had to learn the hard way 'on the job'. The preferred personal weapon at the time was the American M1 carbine, but this was later replaced by a pump-action shotgun for encounters in thick jungle. Men also suffered from sickness, the omnipresent leeches and the humidity. They had to learn how to cope for long periods in the jungle climate, where their uniforms rotted on their bodies and danger lurked constantly. However, for the first time in warfare they did have the benefit of helicopters, both for insertion and for re-supply. Helicopters became a vital tool in the armoury of special forces worldwide.

One of the main problems was the lack of clearings into which to parachute, but it was essential to drop close to CT bases in order to cut off the enemy. Consequently, the SAS developed the art of jumping into the dense jungle canopy and, when the parachute snagged in a tree, each man was equipped with a length of rope down which he could abseil to the ground. This method was not to be found in any airborne forces handbook, and was developed by the men themselves after experimenting on the spot. Another innovation was the

14-day ration pack which did away with heavy cans of food, using dehydrated packets instead, as well as rice to provide bulk.

In 1972, General Gerald Templar took over as British High Commissioner, and soon stamped his personality on the campaign as a whole. It was he who is credited with inventing the concept of 'winning hearts and minds', which has guided British conduct of such brushfire wars ever since. Templar believed that to stand any chance of winning such a conflict it was vital to befriend the local people who could not be defeated by force of arms alone. Templar instituted the building of fortified settlements deep in the jungle where police and special forces patrols could spend lengthy periods of time and be re-supplied by air. The disadvantage was that increasingly the enemy moved north over the border into Thailand where they were safe. At the time it was not government policy to pursue them over the frontier.

In 1953, C Squadron returned to Rhodesia and D Squadron was raised from local volunteers to replace them, command being given to Johnny Cooper, a veteran of the Middle East campaign. Once the building of the jungle forts began, the SAS had to learn to play their part in the hearts and minds policy by learning to live in close proximity with the aboriginal tribes, sharing their customs, and eating their food. British troops could not separate themselves, set up a neat row of tents, install an officers' mess, a cookhouse and a flagpole. The SAS also had to provide medical care for their charges, and the medics had to master the art of basic dentistry and midwifery deep in the jungle.

Cooper led his new squadron on its first patrol to Fort Brooke, a mission that was to last a full 122 days. During that time, half the men had to be evacuated because of sickness, but CT camps were located and destroyed. Cooper and the survivors emerged, their clothes in rags, having withstood a severe ordeal.

The conflict in Malaya was a long drawn-out affair, and was slowly being won by patient police work with help from the army and the SAS patrols. Contacts were few, however, and kills were relatively infrequent in contrast to the numbers of men involved. To get anywhere, days had to be spent hacking a way through the jungle. There were, nevertheless, significant changes afoot which were to put the SAS firmly back into the British Order of Battle. The title Malayan Scouts was dropped and the unit became 22 SAS Regiment, which still exists today. The TA was also expanded with the addition of a further regiment, 23 SAS. It, together with the original 21 SAS, was tasked with operating in an emergency with NATO forces in Germany. A selection and training facility had been established in England under John Woodhouse, but by 1955 it was clear that the back of the insurgency in Malaya had been broken. CTs defected and gave themselves up, tempted by offers of money, while the hardcore hid away in Thailand. The SAS had managed to escape from the clutches of the Parachute Regiment and proudly reverted to wearing their sand-coloured berets.

The end of the conflict brought about a reduction in numbers. The New Zealand Squadron returned home and still remains a part of the SAS family, and a squadron of volunteers from the Parachute Regiment also departed back to their parent regiment, leaving A, B and D Squadrons still conducting patrols in the jungle. However, elsewhere trouble was brewing.

The Jebel Akhdar campaign

The Jebal, known as the 'Green Mountain' lies in the Sultanate of Muscat and Oman at the southern end of the Persian Gulf where it overlooks the Straits of Hormuz and could therefore control the oil tankers plying the Gulf (see Figure 5 on p. 43). Oman was ruled by a hereditary Sultan who had a treaty of friendship with Britain, and a rebellion had broken out by tribes loyal to the religious leader, the Imam. Oman consisted of a fertile coastal strip backed by a mountain ridge, and the rebels were occupying a high plateau, the Jebel Akhdar, which rose to over 1829 m (6,000 feet) and had sheer sides and few paths leading upwards, hardly suitable for conventional infantry.

One of the Sultan's British officers decided to use the SAS, and Colonel Deane-Drummond, then in command of the Regiment, decided to send D Squadron. They were still in the Malayan jungle, but in a typical special forces feat of improvisation, they were pulled back to base, re-kitted, rearmed and were on their way by air all within 48 hours. Arriving in Oman on 9 November 1958, the squadron was under strength but they got down to a serious reconnaissance of their objective. An ancient flight of steps was discovered, which led to the top of the plateau, but which was only wide enough to climb in single file. The squadron, in total darkness, made their way up to the top without alerting the opposition, and sheltered in rock sangars (shelters), sending several men straight back down to collect more water and ammunition. As a demonstration of versatility, that climb was a great feat of stamina for a group of men straight out of the jungle.

D Squadron clung on to their positions on the Jebel plateau and Cairo Radio announced that thousands of British paratroops had been killed. Christmas came and went, at which time it was decided that reinforcements were needed. This entailed pulling A Squadron back from Malaya. More heavy weapons were ferried up to the Jebel, and the squadrons then received support from RAF rocket-firing jets. With the reinforcements, the troops gradually spread out and took control of the plateau. That small campaign demonstrated what a handful of determined men could achieve at minimal cost and proved to the army just what the SAS was capable of.

Redeployment

By March 1959 it was all over in both Malaya and Oman. The remaining two squadrons of 22 SAS returned to Britain and moved into a temporary base at Malvern where they started serious retraining. The Regiment had to decide where its future lay – either in defending the remaining outposts of the British Empire or concentrating on its role with NATO (North Atlantic Treaty Organization) in Europe. Both squadrons were sent regularly to Germany, but faced a four-year pause in active combat. At that time, the SAS was still an air mobile infantry unit. It could put about 160 men into the field at short notice anywhere in the world, from the mountains of Norway to the Far East jungles. In 1960, the Regiment moved to its new permanent base in Hereford, England. The mid-sixties, however, saw new commitments, simultaneously in both Aden and Borneo.

Borneo

The large island of Borneo, from which the Dutch colonists had been expelled, had become an Indonesian province, leaving the two British colonies of Sabah and Sarawak along the northen coast as well as the British protected Sultanate of Brunei. Most of the island was covered by dense jungle and swamps, a climate to which

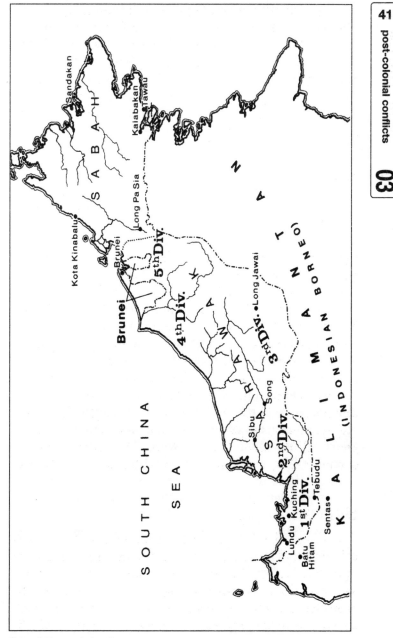

figure 4 Borneo during the emergency

the SAS had become accustomed. Indonesia wished to drive out the remaining British presence in what it regarded as its territory and thus yet another undeclared war flared. Trouble started at the end of 1962 with a local insurrection in Brunei which was suppressed by Gurkas and a Royal Marine Commando unit sent from Singapore, but other insurgences were brewing formented by the Indonesians. SAS A Squadron was sent out and was presented with 1126 km (700 miles) of frontier to patrol, but it made good with the local tribes who provided scouts and a steady flow of intelligence about enemy movements. Small groups of SAS men moved into tribal villages, often for several months at a time, and could then monitor large slices of territory. This again was hearts and minds in action. Still today the Regiment conducts jungle training among its friends in Brunei.

The SAS was rotated squadron by squadron to Borneo, coping with regular incursions over the border by Indonesian patrols. In the background, there were fears that the Vietnam War could spread and engulf other countries in the region. The Regiment was gradually being brought up to strength with the reforming of B Squadron and the addition of G Squadron recruited from the Brigade of Guards. Contacts with the enemy were at first few and far between. The British were not permitted in theory to cross the border, but some SAS patrols did so to gather intelligence. Gradually, however, enemy activity increased as the Indonesians increased their cross-border raids and started to use regular troops. The SAS, although small in number, were proving highly effective – often co-operating with regular Gurkha patrols, backed up by units from the Australian and New Zealand SAS.

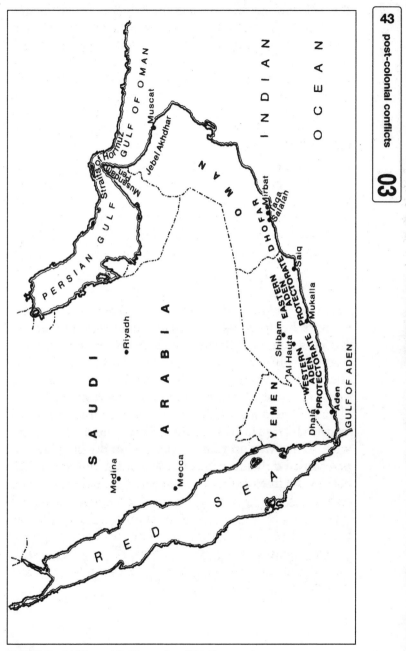

figure 5 Oman, Aden and the Yemen circa 1964–7

Towards the end of 1965, the conflict largely fizzled out, mainly because of political restraints. The SAS found it frustrating not to be able to wage outright war, but the Indonesians had also accepted that Britain was prepared to defend the fledgling Federation of Malaya and Singapore.

Aden

This minnow conflict is interesting because it saw British special forces patrolling in civilian guise for the first time in a combat zone. Between 1964 and 1967, 22 SAS Regiment was involved in fighting in the Aden Protectorate, a country at the mouth of the Red Sea, vastly different from the jungles of Borneo. Consisting mostly of arid mountainous desert and inhabited by a mass of lawless tribes, conflict had already broken out in Yemen to the north and was threatening to spill out into Aden itself, from where Britain had already announced that it would withdraw. The SAS, therefore, inserted small patrols dressed as Arabs into the teeming streets. The patrols were specially trained in pistol shooting and were highly successful in cutting down attacks on British civilians. Otherwise the routine was constant patrolling for the duty squadron in the hills to the north of the town. There was no glory to be won, and when the flag was hauled down, the vacuum was filled by yet another Marxist regime.

Shortly afterwards, the Regiment would find itself back in Oman where it defeated a rebellion against the Sultan, instigated mainly from Yemen, and again succeeded in its hearts and minds approach. After such an unpromising start, the SAS had proved itself, both in the jungle and the desert, as a valuable addition to the army's assets.

04

the origins of the war against terrorism

This chapter will cover:
- how aircraft hijacking became fashionable
- the rise of Middle Eastern and other forms of ethnic terrorism
- early SAS counter-terrorist operations and how the techniques were developed
- the formation of Delta Force.

At the end of the 1960s, special forces in general were casting around for a new role because it was thought that the post-colonial conflicts could be nearing an end as the remaining colonies achieved independence. Little did they know that the SAS Regiment would shortly become involved in a conflict on home ground – the war against Irish terrorism – and in the process would develop special skills that would transform the Regiment from a purely special forces airborne shock infantry unit to the forefront of the war against terrorism. In the early part of the 1970s, the SAS was also embroiled in a counter-insurgency conflict in the undeclared war against rebels in the Sultanate of Oman. Therefore, it has to be borne in mind that this was a busy period for the SAS, which had already started close quarters battle (CQB) training to provide a pool of expert marksmen to act as bodyguards. There was a great demand for their services, both as guards and as trainers for the forces of friendly powers. Individuals and small teams travelled all over the world for a number of years, training bodyguards for wealthy arab rulers. The commitment to the war in Oman reduced the manpower available for such missions, although the training cadre at Hereford in England was maintained. A Counter Revolutionary Warfare (CRW) wing was eventually authorized, with an establishment for one officer, to monitor developments worldwide but this was initially little more than an intelligence-gathering exercise.

Aircraft hijacking as a weapon

Aircraft hijacking was a relatively new phenomenon in the 1960s and one which Western governments were unable to come to grips with. The idea of bringing pressure to bear on governments by hijacking airliners and taking hostages was first used by Fidel Castro's Cuba, mainly by Cubans wishing to escape during the 1950s. However, it became a major problem towards the end of the 1960s when it was employed frequently by various Palestinian groups to blackmail the Israeli government into releasing prisoners. Right from the start, the Israelis refused to negotiate with kidnappers and resorted to armed guards on their airliners, forcing the terrorists to look for softer targets elsewhere. Terrorism was not entirely a purely Palestinian affair; soon others took their cue – a bewildering variety of Italian neo-fascists, Marxist and Maoist urban guerrillas, Japanese radicals, discontented anti-capitalist youths wearing their Che Guevara t-shirts, religious fanatics and even plain criminals. It would be impractical to list all the acronyms employed by the various groups, but outlines are given below of one or two spectacular incidents in which special forces were involved.

Skyjack Sunday

The day of 5 September 1970 was notable for the number of hijackings carried out by the group known as the Popular Front for the Liberation of Palestine (PFLP). Their intention was to free prisoners who were held in West Germany, Britain and Switzerland. Several aircraft were taken and diverted to Dawson's Field, an abandoned RAF strip near Amman in Jordan. Negotiations were entered into using the Red Cross as an intermediary. One hijack was foiled when a security guard shot dead a Nicaraguan leftist on board an El Al aircraft. His companion, a young Palestinian woman, was overpowered by those on board and the flight was diverted to Heathrow where Leila Khalid was arrested. In other hijackings, the governments, with the exception of Israel, simply gave way and agreed to release the prisoners. On 15 September, after the bulk of the hostages had been released and fearing an attack by Israeli special forces, the hijackers evacuated the aircraft and blew them up.

The release of Leila Khalid caused a storm of protest in Britain and a stiffening of government resolve not to give in to terrorist demands in future. The events at the desert airstrip also had the effect of persuading King Hussein of Jordan to eliminate the Palestinian threat to his kingdom. This in turn led to the formation of yet another terror group, Black September, who were shortly to take their revenge in Munich. The month of September used in the group's name commemorated when King Hussein launched his Arab Legion against the Palestinians in Jordan and eliminated their presence in his country. In those early days, the threat of blackmail was all too real but, bit by bit, the hijacking of aircraft became more difficult, and terrorists became deterred by the increased security.

The 1972 Olympic Games massacre

The bloody aftermath of the hostage crisis at the 1972 Olympic Games in Munich was the one event that concentrated minds worldwide on the new threat of organized terrorism. Palestinian guerrillas from the splinter group Black September mounted an attack on the Israeli team quarters, killing two athletes and taking nine hostage. An attempted rescue at a military airfield outside Munich failed, resulting in the deaths of all the hostages, when police opened fire on the vehicles carrying them. The surviving terrorists were flown to Libya, but it is reported that over the years they have been tracked down and terminated by Mossad (The Institute for Intelligence and Special Tasks) agents who do not forget such crimes against Israel.

The Germans had suffered a terrible humiliation and no European government had forces available to counter such a situation. As a result, governments often caved in to terrorists' demands, agreeing to fly them to their safe havens in such countries as Algeria, Iran or Libya. The British government tasked the SAS with preparing a force capable of dealing with incidents in which hostages had been taken, and authorized the expansion of the CRW wing at Hereford. The Germans responded with the foundation of a special unit known as GSG9 (*Grenzschutzgruppe* 9 – Group of Border Control 9), which draws its personnel from the paramilitary frontier police, and the French formed a unit of the *Gendarmerie Nationale* (GIGN), which is described below. Inter-police co-operation was vastly expanded to co-ordinate intelligence-gathering and this information became available to units such as the SAS, which was also briefed by the British Secret Intelligence Service and MI5 (Military Intelligence Section 5).

The European response

Germany – GSG9

GSG9 stands for *Grenzschutzgruppe* 9 and when its formation was organized, it was decided to employ the paramilitary frontier police rather than the army, to avoid accusations of a military elite force akin to the SS (*Schutz Staffeln*). In keeping with their police status, GSG9 operatives, although well-trained as marksmen, have tended to prefer a non-lethal outcome when called upon to react to a situation.

The unit, with an authorized strength of 188 men, started to recruit towards the end of 1972 at a base just outside Bonn, then the Federal Capital, and by the following year it was ready for action. Its first commander was Colonel Ulrich Wegener who maintained close links with the Israelis. The new unit was tasked with hostage rescue but also with protection of VIPs, government installation and even embassies abroad. Originally the unit was subdivided into three operative units, equivalent to SAS squadrons. A fourth was later added, and a further subdivision introduced five-man patrols which form the basic action unit, capable of operating independently or in any combination, known as a SET.

Training, as in all special forces units, is very intense and includes parachuting, combat swimming, marksmanship and high-speed driving. The unit has its own helicopter arm based nearby and, although kept in a high state of alert, it has not been publicly employed to any great extent since the operation in Mogadishu (see p. 55).

France – GIGN

Shortly after the massacre at Munich, terrorists took over the Saudi embassy in Paris and this reportedly led directly to the formation of the GIGN – *Groupe d'Intervention de la Gendarmerie Nationale*. The Gendarmerie is a purely paramilitary police force which answers to the Minister of Defence in France. The new unit, commanded initially by a lieutenant, first consisted of only 15 men divided into three five-man teams, but has since been expanded although it remains relatively small and compact. It has frequently been called upon to act as a Special Weapons and Tactics (SWAT) team within France which helps it to maintain a high level of readiness at all times.

Most other European countries have similar police-based anti-terrorist capability, and there is now much cross-fertilization with intelligence, training and equipment.

Overseas units

Israel

From the time of its creation as the fulfillment of the
Zionist dream of a Jewish homeland, the State of Israel
has been surrounded by hostile neighbours. By
resolutely defending its right to exist it has evoked
admiration in some quarters and bitter enmity in others.
As early as 1953, Israel set up Unit 101 which was a
purely military raiding force tasked with carrying out
strikes deep inside its Arab neighbours from which
Palestinians were infiltrating. Unit 101 gained a
somewhat unsavoury reputation for high-handedness
and, as a result, it was merged with the Israeli Parachute
Battalion, although the policy of cross-border raiding
was continued as was a policy of targeted assassination
of Palestinian leaders. Israel's astounding vistory in the
Six Day War in 1967 did nothing to settle old scores but,
as a direct result, a specialist unit was established known
as the General Staff Reconnaissance Unit 269 or Sayaret
Mackal. This again was a specifically military force of
elite troops, originally some 200 strong, which could be
subdivided into attack units of about 20 men. Later,
when aircraft hijackings became the basic weapons
employed by Palestinians against Israel, men from the
unit were trained as sky marshals and regularly flew
with El Al flights. In December 1968, men of Unit 269,
in typical special forces style, took their war into the
enemy's camp by staging a raid on Beirut Airport where
they blew up 13 Arab airliners as a reprisal.

The Israeli response – the Entebbe rescue

During those early years when SAS squadrons were
being rotated to Oman, and training had to be

maintained for the European war threat, the small CRW capability had little real opportunity to practise its skills, other than to relentlessly rehearse for any eventuality. Contacts, both formal and informal, were maintained with overseas anti-terrorist units, new weapons were tried out and intelligence about potential enemies was collected. Many of the skills learned were put to good use when the commitment to Ulster began in 1976. It is obvious that the Entebbe raid carried out by Israeli commandos in July 1976 was extensively studied by the SAS despite the fact that the Regiment has no official links with Israel. A group from the PFLP hijacked an Air France aircraft and forced the pilot to fly to Entebbe in Uganda where they released 100 passengers but kept a further 106, who were mostly Jewish, hostage. The terrorists were actively supported by the regime of Idi Amin, and the Israelis resolved upon a desperate venture. They flew 3,540 km (2,200 miles) in three Hercules, landed at the airport in an extremely daring and well-planned raid, freed the hostages from the terminal building and destroyed Amin's MIG fighters on the runway. That operation may well have been the prototype for some of the proposed raids during the Falklands War of 1982.

Problems elsewhere

In the Netherlands, the authorities were grappling with the problem of terrorist outrages committed by South Moluccan exiles, and the SAS was called upon for advice and technical assistance. In Germany, the so-called Red Army Faction was waging a bitter guerrilla war against the authorities although many of the guerrilla leaders, including Andreas Baader, had been arrested in 1973. It was this group that indirectly led to the involvement of SAS CRW specialists in a German operation.

The SAS as an anti-terrorist force

As in Ulster in Northern Ireland, the rule of law was still paramount in mainland Britain, where the containment of a terrorist 'incident' was initially a matter for the police, and a military solution was only a final option. Studies were made of the psychology of terrorism, and the subtle techniques of patient negotiation became a powerful weapon in the police armoury. If the military option had to be invoked to save the lives of hostages, the rule was that minimum force should be applied – parameters which still apply today. The paramount aim is to save the lives of the hostages and to ensure that if a gun battle breaks out, innocent civilians do not become caught in the crossfire, which in an urban environment is always a danger. The definition of 'minimum force', however, remains a matter of interpretation and, as in Ulster, a potential minefield. The soldier who is tasked to carry out an operation that may have been sanctioned by politicians, and which the police can no longer handle, can still find himself in the dock accused of murder afterwards.

The SAS was not exactly unprepared to take on the role of developing techniques to counter terrorism. It already had a vast amount of experience in training marksmen for close protection work, which mainly involved highly accurate pistol shooting. To assist their training, a facility that has since become known as 'the killing house' was constructed. In its early days, this was simply a room in which paper targets representing a VIP and potential attackers were placed. The aim was to teach recruits to sort out who was who, and to eliminate the would-be kidnappers. For the new terrorist scenario, the parameters to be considered became more complicated. A group of terrorists could take hostages and hold them in an aircraft, a train, a building or even on a ship. Such a situation could be created by British nationals either as a criminal enterprise or for political ends; or by foreigners applying pressure on the British government or a foreign power. Finally, the situation could take place in Britain or abroad – on British territory or in a foreign country.

The main new technique to be studied was how to gain entry to a space where hostages were being held, and this necessitated much experimentation. Initially, the basic close quarters weapon used was the standard British sub-machine-gun, the Sterling, but this was replaced by the US-made Ingrams. For opening doors, the Remington shotgun, firing a heavy ball to blow off hinges and lock mechanisms, was adopted. In addition, each man carried his own Browning 9 mm Hi-power automatic pistol as a back-up weapon. As soon as entry had been achieved, it was necessary to disorientate the opposition. This led to the development of the stun grenade which is filled with fulminate of mercury and magnesium; the SAS tend to refer to them as 'flash-bangs', an accurate description. The loud explosion and blinding flash can disorientate someone for up to 45 seconds, giving the assault team time to pick their targets and shoot them. Because of fumes in a confined space and the potential use of CS-gas grenades, assault team members wear respirators and a plain zip-front overall. It took several years of patient experimentation to arrive at the present-day high-technology outfit worn by anti-terrorist squads worldwide.

In those early days, the Special Project Team numbered 20 men drawn from all four squadrons, who were trained at the counter-revolutionary warfare (CRW) wing by an officer and four instructors. Their first known deployment was in January 1975 when a civilian airliner was hijacked at Manchester Airport by an Iranian student armed with a pistol. He demanded to be flown to Paris and the pilot agreed to comply. The Special Project

Team were alerted and headed for Stansted Airport near London to set up a reception committee. The hijacker genuinely believed that he had arrived at Paris, and when the SAS stormed the aircraft the man gave himself up. His weapon turned out to be a replica.

In December of that year, the fact that there was an SAS anti-siege unit was announced by the BBC at the instigation of the government. The police had cornered a four-man Provisional IRA team who had entered a flat in Balcombe Street in London after a car chase and a gun battle, and were holding a Mr and Mrs Matthews hostage. With the use of high-technology surveillance equipment, the police were able to eavesdrop on what was happening inside the flat and negotiation was carried out by telephone. The SAS arrived on the scene and the police asked the BBC to insert into a news bulletin the information that they were considering handing over conduct of the operation to the military. The terrorists, who were known to be listening regularly to the radio, promptly decided to give themselves up. This happened before the first full deployment of the Regiment in Ulster, and illustrates the fear that the initials SAS inspired in the ranks of the Provisionals.

SAS missions

The Mogadishu 'incident'

On 13 October 1977, a Lufthansa Boeing 737 en route from Palma to Frankfurt with 86 passengers on board, was hijacked by four terrorists who demanded a ransom of £9 million and the release of members of the Red Army Faction from prison in Germany. A request was made to the British government for SAS assistance for GSG9. This was granted, and two men were selected – Major Alistair Morrison who had led G Squadron to the relief of Mirbat, and Sergeant Barry Davies. They set off for Dubai where the airliner had landed, taking with them a supply of stun grenades, which the Germans did not have.

On arrival, Morrison and Davies met up with the commanding officer of the German unit, Otto Wegener, and two of his men. The rest of his team were in another aircraft, which was still in Turkey where it had followed the terrorists, with the ransom money actually on board. Outside the terminal in searing heat stood the 737 with its frightened passengers on board as Wegener and Morrison struggled to set up an operation to free them. Before they could make an attempt, the Lufthansa jet took off and headed for Aden, where a distinctly unfriendly Marxist government was in place. The Wegener-Morrison team was refused permission to land at Aden but followed the migration of the terrorists to Mogadishu in Somalia, where they met up with the remainder of the GSG9 team. Matters were precipitated when the body of the captain of the hijacked aircraft, who had in fact been murdered in Aden, was thrown out on to the tarmac.

Proof that a hostage has been killed generally triggers an end to the negotiating process and a resort to the military option, as there can be no going back. What Morrison and Davies had practised time and again now had to be put into action, and an attack was approved by the Somali authorities. The job of the SAS team was to effect an entry while the terrorists' attention was diverted by a fire which had been lit on the runway. The assault team climbed silently on to the wings of the jet using rubber-coated ladders and simultaneously blew in the emergency doors on both sides. In went the stun grenades followed by the Germans, who opened fire – above the heads of the hostages who were strapped in their seats. In spite of the duty-free alcohol and aviation spirit which had been spread in the fuselage, there was no fire, and two grenades which were rolled along the floor by the terrorists exploded harmlessly under the well-padded seats. The battle is said to have lasted eight minutes, but it resulted in the death of three hijackers, and the wounding of the fourth, a woman. One German attacker and a hostage were also injured in the operation.

Discreet awards that reflected the British government's satisfaction were made to the two SAS men in the birthday honours list in 1978 – an OBE (Officer of the Order of the British Empire) for Morrison and a BEM (British Empire Medal) for Davies. The successful outcome of the operation did not stop the hijacking of aircraft, but it did at least prove that well-trained and determined assault teams could manage the job without wholesale carnage. In such situations, governments were often in a cleft stick. While they could not be seen to be giving in to terrorist demands, with the subsequent accusations of cowardice in the face of blackmail, neither could they afford a botched release attempt. An aircraft full of dead hostages was an equally grave political impediment and a gift for those journalists who persistently afforded comfort to terrorist organizations.

As a direct result of the Mogadishu operation, the British government ordered an expansion of the CRW role and a full squadron was deployed at Hereford in rotation between tours in Ireland and other training commitments abroad. More money was made available for the purchase of the best equipment on the market, especially in the field of communications. From their German colleagues, the SAS adopted the Heckler and Koch MP5 sub-machine-gun, which is still very much in use today, as their standard close quarters weapon. One-piece flame retardant suits and body armour were adopted, as well as new helmets and respirators with reliable built-in microphones that enabled members to speak to each other.

Obsessive dedication to continuous training is the main hallmark of the SAS, yet there is the danger of boredom setting in if there is no prospect of action, as was the case from 1977 until 1980. By 1980, the 'killing house' consisted of six rooms, with terrorists and hostages being represented by standard NATO paper targets of a charging Russian soldier. There was also a mock-up of the interior of an airliner, and several old aircraft had been assembled on one of the training areas in Wales. The men who were on duty as the instant-readiness team were equipped with bleepers and had to keep their holdall containing assault gear handy at all times. Regular exercises were held which aimed to be as realistic as possible and to cover different situations.

The termination of the Iranian embassy siege in London

The call to action eventually came for the SAS on 30 April 1980. 6 Troop of B Squadron was in the 'killing house' practising standard routines. Splitting into teams of four, they kicked open doors, burst into rooms, fired at targets and afterwards pasted squares of paper over the holes. At 11.48 a.m. the bleepers went off, gear was hastily packed, and the men ran off to be briefed. The reason for the alert was that a telephone call had been received at the 'Kremlin', the SAS operations centre at Hereford, informing the duty officer that a group of terrorists had taken over the Iranian embassy at Prince's Gate, London. The caller was a certain Dusty Gray, an ex-NCO from the regiment who was working as a dog-handler for the Metropolitan Police, and who happened by chance to be outside the embassy. Most accounts state that the SAS team left Hereford and travelled to London on their own initiative, before clearance had been given by the Ministry of Defence. Driving up the motorway in their unmarked Range Rovers, they arrived in the early evening and established a holding area inside Regent's Park Barracks away from prying eyes.

The background to the 'incident' and its ultimate resolution is generally well known, mainly because it was acted out in the full glare of the television cameras. In spite of the distaste felt by the SAS for publicity, one could conjecture that the British government was not exactly displeased. The success had demonstrated to other would-be hostage-takers that Britain was an unhealthy area for such activities, and it increased overseas demand for SAS know-how. The offer of the latter could heighten Britain's political influence all over the world and the know-how could even be sold, at a price.

The bare facts of the matter were as follows. A group of six men, who had been in Britain for several weeks beforehand, had pushed their way into the Iranian embassy, pulled out weapons and claimed to be members of an organization dedicated to independence for Arabistan, an area in the south of Iran inhabited by ethnic Arabs. They took the 26 people in the building hostage, which included two sound technicians from the BBC, a policeman from the diplomatic protection squad and the embassy chauffeur. The remainder were Iranian members of staff.

At that time, the Director of the SAS was Brigadier de la Billière. He had a seat on an organization known as the Joint Operations Centre (JOC) of the Ministry of Defence, which included representatives of the Foreign and Home Offices as well as the intelligence services. The JOC is responsible for activating the SAS but, in the case of a terrorist incident with political connotations, the final say rests with a group called the Cabinet Office Briefing Room (COBRA) which is chaired by the Home Secretary and reports directly to the Prime Minister. At first, however, the incident was a matter for the police, who brought in their experienced team of negotiators and ringed the building with marksmen. They set up headquarters a few doors down from the embassy, in the premises of the Royal School of Needlework. Oan, the leader of the terrorists, demanded an aircraft to take his group, the hostages and an Arab ambassador to an unnamed country. A delicate cat and mouse game then developed, and five hostages were gradually released in exchange for food and an agreement to broadcast Oan's demands on BBC networks.

For the team planning the eventual assault, the building was unknown territory but luckily the British caretaker proved to be a mine of information. In addition, Chris Cramer, one of the BBC men taken hostage, was released on account of illness and could be carefully debriefed. A plywood model was constructed. One thing that was discovered was that the ground-floor and first-floor windows were armour plated and could not simply be smashed through with sledgehammers; explosive charges would be needed.

The following evening the assault team members were moved out from the barracks in hired vans, and established themselves in a new holding area in a side street near the target building. For them, the waiting began as negotiations continued. On the night of 2 May, a reconnaissance was made across the rooftops of Prince's Gate to reach number 16 (the Iranian embassy), where it was discovered that a skylight could be opened. From then on, however, it was still a question of waiting for the negotiated release of the hostages, or for the terrorists to decide to kill someone. By the morning of Monday 5 May, the atmosphere in the holding area was becoming claustrophobic, the only relief being a chance to jog in Hyde Park. But at 1.45 p.m., the situation suddenly altered when three shots (in some accounts, two) were heard from inside the embassy. Oan, the terrorists' leader, had carried out his threat: he had killed a hostage. Final proof came at 7 p.m. when the body of the Iranian press attaché was dumped outside the front door of the embassy. From then on, matters had to be resolved. At 7.07 p.m. precisely, the senior policeman signed a handwritten sheet of paper and handed it to Colonel Mike Rose, the commanding officer of 22 SAS.

Although the negotiator continued to talk to Oan on the telephone about arrangements for a coach to take the terrorists to the airport, the command of the operation was now in the hands of the military. Ever since the shots had been heard, the assault team had been on full alert and had moved into number 14, the premises of the Royal College of Physicians next door to the embassy. All the equipment had been prepared, weapons were loaded and the final briefing had been carried out. The aim was to create a diversion at the front while entry was effected at the rear, with teams entering the ground floor via the garden, and others abseiling down on to the first-floor balcony. At 7.23 p.m., demolition charges went off at the front and CS gas was pumped into the building through the broken windows. As the ground-floor assault team ran into position with shaped charges to smash the windows, they saw above them the inert form of one of their comrades, a Fijian, who was caught up in his abseil harness. If they used explosives they would kill him, yet he was in danger of being roasted alive in the flames that were licking through the window. He was cut down and, despite his injuries, went inside with his team. The men below used a sledgehammer to open the door and they too charged in, with Soldier 'I' (his identification at the subsequent inquest) in the lead.

The adrenalin was making me feel confident, elated. My mind was crystal clear as we swept on through the library and headed towards our first objective. I reached the head of the cellar stairs first, quickly joined by Sek and two of the call signs. The entry to there was blocked by two sets of step-ladders. I searched desperately with my eyes for any signs of booby-traps. There wasn't time for a thorough check. We had to risk it. We braced ourselves and wrenched the ladders away.

The team on the first floor rushed up the stairs to the second floor where the hostages were being held, while the ground-floor men systematically cleared the lower part of the building. There was total confusion: firing from the sub-machine-guns; women screaming; smoke billowing; the concussions of stun grenades; and clouds of tear gas. The assault team, encumbered with heavy body armour and their respirators misty from perspiration, moved automatically, assessing and reacting. Oan was on the first-floor landing but before he could shoot, the policeman, P.C. Lock, wrestled him to the floor. An SAS man shouted at the policeman to move out of the way and dispatched the terrorist with a burst from his Heckler and Koch. Elsewhere, terrorists had started to shoot wildly, killing a hostage and wounding two or three others before the rescuers burst in. The terrorists threw their weapons away and tried to mingle with the hostages as the SAS yelled for them to be pointed out. Two were killed instantly and another was dispatched by the team on the ground floor.

In 11 very long minutes, the action was over. A line of assault team members formed on the stairs and bundled the hostages, none too gently, down to the back lawn where they were thrown to the ground, tied up and held at gunpoint. Suddenly there was a shout as one of the people coming down the stairs was identified as a terrorist. Soldier 'I' saw him – and that he had a fragmentation grenade clutched in his fist. Soldier 'I' could not fire, as his mates at the bottom of the stairs were in his line of sight:

I've got to immobilise the bastard. I've got to do something. Instinctively, I raised the MP 5 above my head and in one swift, sharp movement brought the stock of the weapon down on the back of his neck. I hit him as hard as I could. His head snapped backwards and for one fleeting second I caught sight of his tortured hate-filled face. He collapsed forward and rolled down the remaining few stairs, hitting the carpet in the hallway, a sagging, crumpled heap. The sound of two magazines being emptied into him was deafening.

In fact, the pin was still in the grenade that the terrorist had held. Then the order came crackling though the men's headphones to abandon the building as it was on fire. Back in number 14, they stripped off their assault kit as the adrenalin rush ebbed away. A few minutes later they were outside, bundling themselves into the hired vans, having handed over their weapons to the police for forensic examination. They were driven back to Regent's Park Barracks where there was time for justifiable self-congratulation and the task of emptying cans of beer that had been thoughtfully provided. The celebrations were interrupted by the arrival of the Prime Minister, Margaret Thatcher, accompanied by her husband. She was obviously delighted and took the time to move around the room speaking to everyone. The men sat down to watch the events on television, then it was back to Hereford. The Fijian abseiler had been taken to a hospital in Fulham, but that night he was abstracted by the SAS and flown back to base in a helicopter. In spite of being quite badly burnt, he made a full recovery. Of the terrorists, only one had survived; he had been discovered wounded among the hostages when they were sorted out on the lawn.

A number of writers and journalists have stated that it was made quite clear to the SAS that they were to take no prisoners. Governments had long since come to realize that putting terrorists in prison could often lead to further hostage-taking by members of their group endeavouring to exert pressure for their release. It is unlikely that we will ever know if such orders were actually given to the SAS as the authorities would not admit to flouting the so-called rule of law. The British press generally welcomed the outcome, although there was some comment about the fact that several of the hostages stated that the SAS had killed the terrorists after they had surrendered. The job of the assault team was to rescue hostages and remove them from the premises as quickly as possible; there is no time for niceties such as requesting people to surrender. It was known in advance that the enemy were armed, and they had proved that they were prepared to kill if their demands were not met. They had also stated that they had explosives in the building and would blow it up if attacked. It is obvious that they had to be killed before they had a chance to do further mischief, and this is what such SAS teams are taught to do in the 'killing house'. Some months later, four of the SAS concerned had to give evidence at an inquest, which turned into a game with the media as the latter tried frantically to get photographs. The soldiers gave their evidence, identifying themselves only by letters, and in due course a verdict of justified killing was pronounced by the jury.

As far as the Regiment was concerned, it wished to sink back into obscurity and get on with the round of tours in Northern Ireland and with training for the next 'incident'. As a spin-off from the Iranian embassy media coverage, a record number of would-be volunteers applied to join TA units, and speculation about the role of the Regiment refused to die away.

A foiled coup attempt

Just over a year later, while Britain was celebrating the marriage of the Prince of Wales, the SAS received another call. One of the guests at the royal wedding was Dawda Kairaba Jawara, President of the Gambia, a small ex-British colony in West Africa. Some Marxist-oriented rebels used his absence to stage a coup, seizing vital installations in Banjul, the capital, including the airport. Although small, the country was a successful democracy, had no standing army, and remained in the British sphere of influence. News of events reached the Foreign Office on 30 July 1981, and urgent consultations were held with Washington and Paris, since both the USA and France had an interest in the region. As a result, Hereford was alerted, where Major Ian Crooke was on duty in the absence of Colonel Rose.

According to accounts published at the time, Crooke was ordered to take whatever he needed and to get to the scene. For some reason, never explained, the duty Special Projects Team was not employed and the RAF was not ordered to provide a Hercules plane. Crooke gathered up two other men and, with holdalls packed with weapons, explosives and a portable satellite telephone, they flew to Paris. There, they boarded a routine Air France flight to Banjul, the problem of their luggage having been solved discreetly by an employee of the British embassy who arranged diplomatic passage through the security checks. In Banjul itself, a squad of French-trained troops had arrived from neighbouring Senegal and had retaken the airport, where they had been joined by the President who had flown in from London. This raises the question of why Crooke and his team had not travelled with the President. On arrival, Crooke discovered that the hostages were being held 11 km (7 miles) outside the town, but other than that, nobody seemed to be taking any form of initiative.

Now comes the fantastic bit. The three SAS men, fully armed, made their way through the lines of rebel troops surrounding the airport and into town, where they knocked on the door of the British embassy. There they found the ambassador, who was having to evade sporadic gunfire, and discovered that one of the President's wives together with her four children had been taken to a hospital in the town. They moved on to the hospital and, while Crooke posing as an unarmed bystander engaged the guards on the gate in conversation, his two colleagues crept up and overpowered the guards. They released the prisoners, delivered them to the safety of the embassy and then discovered that the Senegalese, poorly led, had attempted to break out from the airfield and had been beaten back. Undeterred, Crooke led his small team back, gathered a group of Senegalese and staged a counter-attack. In four days, he and his men broke the back of the resistance and captured the leadership.

Meanwhile the Americans, smelling a Libyan plot, had alerted their Delta Force (see p. 74) who had flown into Dakar, the capital of Senegal. The State Department then got cold feet and left them there. The British Foreign Office also panicked, but Hereford, with Nelsonian blindness, stated that they had lost contact with Crooke's team, which was quite untrue as they had a satellite phone. In the end, there was quiet satisfaction with the outcome, discreet awards were no doubt made, and Britain retained a staunch friend in a volatile region. The Gambian mission was a classic example of a few men inserted into the right place, with initiative and determination, being able to master a fluid situation.

Peterhead prison

From time to time the SAS has been asked by the British Home Office to test the security of prisons by attempting to break in, and they carry out similar exercises at such establishments as nuclear power stations. On 3 October 1987, however, they had to do it for real, at the top-security Victorian Peterhead prison in Aberdeen. Four days previously, a group of three inmates, one of them a convicted murderer, had taken a prison officer hostage and from time to time had paraded him on the roof, threatening him with a hammer. The authorities had instigated a negotiating process which was getting nowhere. Presumably they felt that sending in a riot squad of police or prison personnel could lead to the hostage being injured or even killed. In the pitch darkness of early morning, witnesses heard a shouted 'Let's go!' from inside the compound. One group of SAS men threw stun grenades and tear gas into the wing as an assault team abseiled down from the roof and entered through a window. Five explosions were heard and smoke billowed out through a hole in the roof that had been made by the prisoners. It was all over in seconds and the hostage was released unharmed. Had the prisoners had firearms, the outcome would probably have been different, but the Peterhead operation does prove that an SAS attack need not necessarily be lethal.

The Gibraltar shoot-out

The final operation to be discussed in this chapter certainly was lethal. What started out as the simple termination of three known IRA terrorists in Gibraltar in the spring of 1988 was to end up with the British government and their executive arm, the SAS, in the international dock. The matter was extensively aired in the media at the time, and much has since been written about it. By its ineptitude, the government handed the IRA a propaganda victory and once again reopened the whole question of a 'shoot to kill' policy. The affair ended up in the European Court, as the relatives of the deceased were awarded compensation from the British government, and this provoked quite a howl of rage in several sections of the press. As a sub-plot to the main drama, there was trial by television; and when some of the evidence presented was found to be flawed, there was criticism of television reporting itself. An increasingly paranoid government attempted to gag the press, which only made matters worse. The facts of the case were relatively simple. A well-known IRA member and suspected bomb-maker, Sean Savage, had been located in Spain in the autumn of 1987, as had Daniel McCann, by trade a butcher and accomplished terrorist. An extensive intelligence-gathering operation then got underway, and at the beginning of 1988 an MI5 (UK Security Service) team was sent to Gibraltar. By this time, the experts were fairly certain that the terrorists' target was to be the resident military band which performed the ceremony of changing the guard outside the governor's residence in the colony. There was also disquiet about the fact that the IRA had perfected a remote-controlled detonating device that could be activated by pushing a button in a coat pocket. On 4 March, Savage and McCann arrived at Malaga Airport where they were joined by a woman, Mairead Farrell, who had a long record of terrorist offences. It was a star team that the IRA had assembled, in revenge for Loughgall perhaps, and nobody could pretend that they were there to enjoy a holiday in the sun.

The Spanish police had been briefed on what was thought to be afoot, yet through ineptitude they lost trace of the bombers as they left the airport. Their men were still doing the rounds of hotels, showing pictures of the suspects a couple of days after all three were dead. Two days earlier on 2 March, intelligence indicated that the operation was imminent, as a fourth member of the team, a woman, had made several trips to the Rock to scout the area where the military band performed. The JOC in London assessed the situation and authorized the deployment of a troop-sized (16-man) SAS team, which included an explosives expert. They flew out on 3 March. In charge on the spot was Joseph Canepa, the Gibraltar police commissioner and, from all the evidence, there has never been anything to suggest that his orders were anything other than to apprehend the terrorists.

The operation was given the code name Favius. In a thorough briefing to all concerned, Canepa stated that the object was to arrest the terrorists, disarm them and make the bomb safe. The assumption was that a car bomb would be used, parked in the small square where the band assembled before the performance, and that it would be detonated by remote control. All the SAS men involved stated that it was stressed to them most emphatically that it would be a push-button detonator. It was also assumed, quite naturally, that the terrorists would be armed.

So far, all seemed relatively straightforward. With hindsight we know that the three were unarmed, that the bomb was still in a car park in Marbella, and that they intended to use a timing device to detonate it. Had that information been available, the local police could have handled the affair and all three would be behind bars, still alive.

On the afternoon of Sunday 6 March, watchers were deployed around the town. Among them were four members of the SAS team, working in pairs. Each man was wearing denims and a lightweight jacket with a Browning 9 mm pistol tucked into the waistband of his trousers. Small radios with microphones hidden in the lapels of the jackets ensured adequate communications. The reception committee was in place and waiting.

Savage was seen to approach a white Renault 5 parked in the square where the band would assemble, open the door and 'fiddle with something inside' – which effectively signed the terrorists' death warrants. As he loitered near the car, Farrell and McCann were picked up walking into the town from the Spanish border post.

Soldier 'G', (the operatives were identified only by letters at the subsequent inquest), the explosives expert, was sent out from the operations room to examine the car, but would have been well aware of the probability that it was booby-trapped. There were no outward signs of uneven springs denoting a heavy weight inside, but although it was a relatively new vehicle, it was fitted with a rusty aerial, which might have indicated that it had been tampered with. On that basis, it was felt that the car could contain a remote-control bomb, and at 3.40 p.m. Canepa signed the authorization for the military to take responsibility for the operation. At that time all three terrorists were walking together northwards towards the Spanish border, followed by the four soldiers. Then, for some reason, Savage separated and started to walk back in the direction of the town, which caused those shadowing the trio to split. Soldiers 'A' and 'B' continued behind McCann and Farrell while 'C' and 'D' stuck with Savage.

Just before 4 p.m., a local police inspector, who was not aware of the operation, was called back to base as his car was required – ironically, to take the arrested terrorists to prison. Owing to the heavy traffic he switched on his siren. This seems to have alarmed the trio, who became noticeably jumpy. McCann turned his head and made eye contact with Soldier 'A', who was about 10 m (33 feet) behind him. In evidence, the soldier said that he was about to issue a challenge as he pulled out his pistol, when McCann moved his hand across his body. Assuming that the man was going for the button,

Soldier 'A' fired one round into McCann's back and then, seeing Farrell make a movement towards her bag, he shot her too with a single round. As he fired again at McCann, Soldier 'B' fired at Farrell and then also at McCann. Hearing the shots, Savage spun round and Soldier 'C' shouted 'Stop!' As he did so, he noticed his target make a movement towards his pocket. Both soldiers opened fire. At 4.06 p.m., Soldier 'F', the SAS officer in charge of the team, relinquished military control.

At first it had all seemed quite simple. An active service unit consisting of three ruthless IRA members, caught in the act of planting a bomb which could have killed hundreds of innocent bystanders, had been eliminated. The tone of Monday's newspaper headlines was one of jubilation, but that afternoon in the House of Commons the then Foreign Secretary, Sir Geoffrey Howe, made a statement concerning the affair on behalf of the British government. He laid out the facts as known but said that the white Renault did not actually contain a bomb and that the three dead IRA members were unarmed at the time. The bomb was not discovered until the following day in a car parked in Marbella.

The government found itself on the defensive, forced to explain the apparent cold-blooded killing of the terrorists, and the SAS was accused of being Thatcher's assassins with a 007-type 'licence to kill'. The press went on the rampage, attempting to dig up every possible detail of the shootings, and printed the Spanish police version of their side of the operation. The Spanish police flatly denied that they had lost the terrorists at Malaga Airport, and claimed they had shadowed them all the way to the Gibraltar border. What had originally been a disaster for the IRA, turned into a triumph: they had three new martyrs to mourn, and every movement of the soldiers concerned was analysed second by second.

Allegations by witnesses and supposed witnesses were printed which stated that the SAS pumped shots into their victims when they were already on the ground. Father Raymond Murray gives a detailed analysis of the general press coverage in his book, *The SAS In Ireland* (Mercier Press, 1990). He states that having shot the three IRA members dead in the head and back from a close range in cold blood, the British prepared their defence: first, by misinforming the British media, tabloid and broadsheet alike; and second, by delaying the inquest to September on a flimsy excuse in order to cool the atmosphere, to give more time for misinformation and to attempt to intimidate key witnesses. Father Murray, who attended the funeral mass for Mairead Farrell, went on to state that the alleged worry about a press-button detonator for the bomb was a 'classic *post-hoc* invention'.

Here, the intention is to provide a history of special forces and not a critique of British government policy. The rules of engagement for the operation, which were furnished to the coroner and are thus in the public domain, are probably similar to those for missions in Ulster and on the UK mainland. They authorize the operatives to 'open fire against a person if you have reasonable grounds for believing he/she is currently committing, or is about to commit, an action which is likely to endanger your or their lives, or the life of any person, and if there is no way to prevent this.'

If the suspicion about a 'button job' was not a complete government invention after the event, which seems unlikely, then it was the job of the SAS to eliminate the threat by killing the terrorists once they became alarmed. Otherwise, why were they sent there in the first place? If it was simply a government plot to kill the terrorists, why do so using four unmasked men in plain clothes, in broad daylight on a busy thoroughfare?

The two-week inquest ended on 3 September 1988 and, by a majority of nine to two, the jury brought in a verdict of lawful killing. This satisfied the government as well as a large section of British public opinion which had been annoyed by the efforts of the lawyer representing the families of the dead trio to blacken the SAS men. The SAS members had to endure a lengthy grilling in the witness box simply for carrying out their duty. If any 'secret' orders had been given, then surely those responsible for them should have been called, rather than the soldiers? Yet however much the Regiment may deplore the harsh glare of publicity, the fact remains that they are subject to the rule of law and there is little the government can do to protect them. Other countries use specially trained police units for counter-terrorist work, but Britain has chosen a military option, which places soldiers in a difficult position. They are essentially trained to wage war rather than to do police work, and if the government sends members of the SAS fully armed on to the street, it should shoulder the responsibility.

Gibraltar is probably not the last time that the CRW team will go into action, and they are still there, training relentlessly. From its post-war origins as a specialist infantry unit employed in fighting brushfire wars abroad, the SAS has become the world's elite anti-terrorist unit. Although regarded by some sections of the British community as bogeymen, the fact that the SAS are there ensures a high level of deterrence to any would-be terrorists who might decide to operate on British soil.

Delta Force

In the summer of 1962, a young special forces officer, Charles Beckwith, serving at Fort Bragg, North Carolina, was seconded for a year to serve with the SAS. In his book, *Delta Force: The Army's Elite Counterterrorist Unit* (Avon, 2000), he describes his impressions of life at Hereford, and it is clear he became an ardent fan. He liked the lack of rigid discipline, the relaxed relationship between officers and other ranks and the emphasis placed on individual initiative.

Once back at Fort Bragg, he began a campaign for an SAS-style unit, but his recommendations fell on deaf ears. The US military thought they were good and saw no need to change their style whatsoever. Beckwith was ignored and spent the following years in Vietnam with special forces units.

Back at Fort Bragg in 1974, Beckwith discovered that the new commander was a supporter of his, and together they submitted a new paper to higher headquarters. Thus followed two hard years of bargaining for the idea of a small specialist unit to deal with aircraft hijackings and hostage situations, overcoming resistance from other units such as the navy SEALS and Rangers who fought to defend their territory. However, in 1977, Beckwith was authorized to form the 1st Special Forces Operations Detachment – Delta, known as Delta Force. The initial establishment called for 1,200 men, subdivided into seven-man troops which could be further broken down into four or even two-man patrols. The emphasis was on the use of initiative and the usual skills such as parachuting, weapons and driving vehicles.

Beckwith was given space at Fort Bragg and set about preparing a headquarters and working out budgets prior to gaining formal recognition. In the background, the army Chief of Staff had grown cool on the whole idea, and Beckwith and his team found themselves working in a vacuum. However, the successful culmination of the Mogadishu rescue prompted President Carter to enquire what forces the USA had to deal with a similar situation. Nobody dared to tell the President, but then someone remembered the four-month-old Beckwith report and Beckwith was summoned to Washington to be told that he had the authority to activate Delta.

That should have settled the matter, but Beckwith became embroiled in the usual inter-service rivalries and vested interests. Beckwith's unit was derisively nicknamed 'Charlie's Angels' after the popular television series. Other units questioned the need for a different approach, and claimed that Beckwith would poach their best men. Eventually, most of the opposition was overcome and Beckwith was given two years to set up the unit. He was, nevertheless, encumbered with an unworkable chain of command: forced to go through the Fort Bragg hierarchy, then an airborne corps HQ, the Department of the Army, and the Joint Chiefs before getting access to the President.

Selection and training was finally underway, much of it along the lines of SAS models, stressing endurance. Delta, though, was not a complete clone of the SAS and owed much to the style of its founder and commander, Colonel Beckwith, as well as to Dick Meadow, another Vietnam special forces veteran who had been to Hereford. Only seven out of the first 30 recruits made it through the whole process.

Operation Eagle Claw

The newly formed and, as yet, untried Delta Force was soon to face its baptism of fire and to become entangled in what would result in a debacle. On 4 November 1979, a mob of Iranian students and revolutionary guards stormed the American embassy in Teheran, took 63 members of staff hostage and captured a huge haul of highly sensitive documents. The attackers were fanatical followers of the ageing Ayatollah Khomeini who had replaced the Shah of Iran in a coup and inaugurated the Islamic Republic theocracy. The conditions for the release of the US diplomats was the return from the US of the hospitalized Shah to face 'revolutionary justice', which was not going to be granted. In Washington it was realized that there was little chance of negotiation with the Iranians and that something, therefore, had to be done.

Beckwith was given the job of working out a rescue plan. This was far from easy owing to the extreme distance involved, the lack of US bases in the area, and the lack of intelligence available as the remaining CIA people were among the hostages. However, by December a plan had been formulated. In outline, it involved flying the team in by helicopter to a desert strip, then on to a further strip closer to Teheran, taking trucks into town and assaulting the compound. Having freed the hostages, the team would exfiltrate and fly the hostages out in C-130s. A mock-up of the embassy compound was built, and Delta practised every move intensely, keeping well out of the sight of the media.

At that stage, things started to snowball out of control. The original US Navy pilots selected to fly the helicopters proved unsuitable and had to be replaced by pilots from the US marines. Tanker aircraft had to be provided at the first staging post, known as Desert One, to refuel the helicopters, which meant extra men to guard them, swelling the numbers required for the mission to 120. This in turn required two extra helicopters, the pilots of which had to be trained.

Intelligence started to improve, and Dick Meadow and a small team went into Teheran. The CIA located an airstrip beside a road to the south of the city, and discovered the sand was firm enough to support the weight of heavy transport aircraft. The final plan emerged by mid-January and called for eight Sea Stallion helicopters to be launched from a carrier stationed in the Gulf. In addition, six C-130 transporters would be employed to fly in from Egypt, three of them loaded with fuel, and would rendezvous at night at Desert One. Rangers were attached to guard the various sites as well as an air force team to supervise the refuelling operation. All the armed services thus had a slice of the action, which kept everyone happy. Meadows and his team had organized trucks to take in Delta from the second staging post and bring them out together with the released hostages. This was Murphy's Law in the making – if it can go wrong, it will go wrong. Successful special operations are planned on the basis of 'keep it simple, stupid' (KISS).

Anger was mounting in the USA about America's humiliation, and President Carter was up for re-election. The hostages were regularly paraded before the TV cameras, and the President had to be seen to be doing something. On 15 April 1980, when the various elements of the assault force were assembled, President Carter was briefed about the final plan and approved the operation. The Delta team left Fort Bragg five days later en route for Egypt. There the assault team assembled, 90 from Delta, some special forces men from Bad Tolz, and Rangers and Iranian dissidents. After a short rest, their C-130s took off again and flew a zig-zag course through the gaps in the Iranian radar chain to land at Desert One. While everyone was clambering out, lights were seen coming down the road parallel to the runway and a bus full of passengers came into view, which failed to stop until shots had been fired to blow out a tyre. While the bus passengers were being searched, another vehicle appeared, a fuel tanker. It refused to stop and a Ranger fired a grenade at it causing it to explode in a fireball that could be seen for miles.

Meanwhile, the eight helicopters had taken off from the carrier but, as they entered Iranian airspace, the weather clamped down and reduced visibility. One of them was forced to land when a warning light came on, and was abandoned by the crew. Another was forced to return to the carrier when its instruments failed. Beckwith was down to the bare minimum, six, to carry out his mission. When yet another helicopter was forced to return, the decision was made to abort the mission. The men began to embark the C-130s as the helicopters were still refuelling. One of the helicopters managed to crash into a C-130 starting a major fire. Several of the crew of the two aircraft died in the fire while those on the ground clambered into the remaining transport and headed back to a base in Oman. The marine pilots simply abandoned the helicopters at Desert One.

The embattled Carter went on television and accepted full responsibility, but the recriminations had already started and Charlie Beckwith was the obvious scapegoat. It is easy to be wise after the event, but with such a tangled chain of command and competencies, failure was inevitable. Beckwith left the army under a cloud and Carter failed to be re-elected.

05

selection and training in the SAS

This chapter will cover:
- where special forces personnel come from
- the rigours of selection
- the scope of special forces.

The preceding chapters have shown the wide variety of operational situations in which the SAS Regiment has been involved since 1947, ranging from steaming tropical jungles to the deserts of Arabia. What is evident is the adaptability required: all ranks must be able to cope with whatever may be flung at them, often at short notice. A troop can be pulled off a mountain in Norway, flown back to Hereford in England, be re-kitted and be on its way to Iraq in 24 hours. Of course there will be griping from all concerned, but that is endemic to all armies and soldiers the world over. The SAS, however, will simply make the best of things, work out what needs to be done and then get on with it.

There is no such thing as the typical SAS recruit – whether officer, sergeant or trooper – and they vehemently deny that they are in any way supermen. By the very nature of the job they do, they tend to lead somewhat restricted lives, ever wary of publicity, but they also get married, have children, buy houses and pay tax. The Regiment has thrown up remarkably few absolute rogues, has its own ways of weeding out the potentially undesirable, and fosters a strong sense of internal loyalty. The SAS is elitist but does not need to brag about the fact, and in ethical terms it could be likened to the medieval war band in which allegiance was based upon ability, mutual trust and the feeling of being part of a 'family' – nobody can lead except by example.

Recruitment

The regular Regiment recruits from those already serving within the British army, while the territorial Regiments find their volunteer members from the civilian population. Having said that there is no typical SAS recruit, certain generalizations can be made based upon empiric observation. A high degree of individuality and self-reliance is certainly called for, coupled with the ability to get on with others in both small and large formations. An SAS member has to be able to sit in a hole for several weeks with two or three colleagues, with little chance of movement, and not harbour murderous thoughts about someone else's annoying habits. Very few lengthy orders are given – a problem is stated and it is up to the individual or small squad to sort out how to solve it. He must be able to operate entirely alone without waiting for an officer or a non-commissioned officer (NCO) to tell him what to do. He must of course be extremely fit, but not necessarily in the muscle-bound sense. A form of mental toughness and a highly developed strength of will is needed; a determination never to give up. In addition, a balanced psychological profile is essential to produce someone who is even-tempered and unlikely to get in a panic when things start going wrong. They need to trust their mates, and to have absolute confidence in them in any circumstances. On top of all these character traits, one vital attribute is the possession of a strong sense of humour – often of the black variety.

There is no room in the Regiment for the thug or the gorilla – violence and the ability to kill are part of the job, but that is all. An officer who had commanded the SBS once told me that he had only had to get rid of one man, because that man had developed an unhealthy interest in killing people. The SAS do not brawl around the pubs and brag in bars about their exploits – anybody who does is a candidate for immediate RTU (return to unit). Many of those I have met have an intellectual curiosity, a high degree of intelligence, and a practical approach to life with an immense zest for living it to the full. Often small and stocky, they have watchful eyes and the restfulness often associated with advanced practitioners of martial arts. David Stirling, an aristocrat by birth, envisaged the SAS as a classless society, which is what it has become, where position in the pecking order is determined by ability rather than by the automatic respect due to rank. The British army has often been accused of racism, but in the SAS the criteria for acceptance is passing selection and having ability. Several men from different ethnic backgrounds have become senior NCOs, and it is obvious that positive discrimination would not have had a role to play in their promotion.

The selection process

The process of selection laid down by John Woodhouse in the 1950s has changed very little. Essentially selection involves a number of hikes of ever-increasing length over difficult terrain, advanced map-reading skills referred to as 'land navigation', and the carrying of heavier and heavier loads to prove an individual's stamina and powers of endurance over a three-week period. Both officers and other ranks undergo the same ordeal, although for the former there is an extra week at the end known as officers' week. Here, those who have successfully completed the first parts have to prepare and explain a variety of tactical problems to an often highly critical audience which will include senior officers and experienced NCOs.

In the past, the course has been criticized for being over-physical, but that is the system which has worked well for the SAS. The failure rate is immensely high – a figure of around 80 per cent has been quoted – but the Regiment has always resolutely refused to water down its standards for acceptance. A series shown on British BBC television (2001) gave a fascinating glimpse into the selection methods used by the SAS. It was called *Are you tough enough?* and featured a group of around 20 'volunteers', all of whom were civilians and pre-eminent in their particular sport disciplines. They were carefully picked and taken out to Namibia, a particularly harsh desert environment, where they were put under the control of a group of ex-SAS members, presided over by a pugnacious staff-sergeant known as Eddie. He put the group of volunteers, all of them fit and highly motivated young men and women, through a crash course of military discipline. Over a couple of weeks of intensive work, they were whittled down to a final group of four who had to learn free-fall parachuting and were then sent off to rescue a 'hostage'.

Over the years, several men have died from exposure up on the Welsh hills, but that is a risk that is accepted as the price for excellence. Once through basic selection, the potential recruit faces several more months of continuation training when they can still be sent back to their parent formation at any time. Only then are they 'badged' and admitted to a squadron, yet still on probation.

The outsider may well ask: why do it? The average recruit is in their mid-twenties, has a good military record and is already an NCO, although they will revert to the rank of trooper when they try for the SAS. The Regiment does provide information and gives presentations to various army units, but it is up to the individual to make the effort to apply for selection, which takes place twice annually in the formidable range of bleak mountains known as the Brecon Beacons in Wales. Participants on the winter course face the hazards of mist, snow and almost continual dampness, while those who opt for the summer course have to cope with the sweaty heat.

Owing to their part-time status, selection for the TA candidates is spread out over a longer period, but is just as gruelling; they are not second-class SAS. Many are looking for a sense of adventure and personal challenge which they find lacking in a normal army environment – there are no great financial inducements.

An SAS recruit has to be recommended by their commanding officer who is generally unwilling to lose a promising young soldier, and so can make difficulties about processing the application. The soldier has to weigh up the potential risk to his career by trying for the SAS and then failing, as well as the risk to any personal relationships of having to spend up to eight months in every year separated from his family. Today the British army is in the process of retrenchment, which means that skilled personnel are in even greater demand as older and more experienced men are made redundant. Against that, although reverting to the ranks, the soldier in the SAS will receive extra pay and, after their probationary period can expect to be enrolled as a permanent member, spending the rest of their career with the Regiment. Many senior NCOs take commissions later on in their careers and can serve as officers in a variety of capacities.

An officer also has to consider their career when thinking about applying. The army as a whole looks upon a tour with the SAS favourably but individual regiments and corps may think differently. Service with the SAS has not hindered certain officers, for example, General de la Billière, from rising to extremely high rank, and on acceptance there is the reward of promotion to captain as there are no subalterns in the Regiment. Some officers who join are content with a tour as a troop commander and then go on to different things but others, obviously bitten by the bug, return as majors to command squadrons and then aspire to a regimental command as a lieutenant-colonel.

On arrival at Hereford, equipped with the necessary approvals, each potential recruit is given a thorough medical check-up and has to pass the standard British Army Fitness for Battle test – which, surprisingly enough, means a 10 per cent reduction in the numbers on the course right from the start. The really determined candidates will have been working on their own intensive fitness programme for weeks or months in advance. They come from a variety of parent units, but there is said to be a preponderance of recruits from the Parachute Regiment and the Light Infantry. G Squadron still recruits from the Brigade of Guards, although it is no longer exclusive, and there will be others from the Artillery, the Engineers and other army formations. There is no shouting of orders and, to a large extent, the candidates have to sort themselves out. They are issued with basic kit and told when to report and where – if they are not there, the trucks leave without them and they receive a railway warrant back to whence they came. There is no 'bull', standing to attention by beds, marching along shouting slogans or being 'beasted' over assault courses by screaming NCOs.

The staff of the Training Wing, according to accounts, can be quite remote and cynical – almost detached from the process, as if they simply do not care. What they are doing, however, is carefully assessing how each candidate is doing, judging not only their level of stamina but whether they will 'fit in'. Much of the first week is taken up with instruction in land navigation, for many of the recruits come from units where such skills are not normally practised. In the SAS, map references have to be memorized for security reasons, and maps must be carried folded along the original creases to avoid giving the enemy any indication of the precise operational area. The rest of the time the candidates work as a group on a series of gradually increased hikes across the hills to build up their level of fitness.

During the second week, the pace hots up, the loads and distances increase, as does the amount of time each man has to spend out on the hills. This inevitably takes its toll: more and more candidates are either rejected or resign voluntarily. There are also those who have to be put aside on medical grounds, but they at least can come back and have another go. The day starts at four o'clock in the morning as sleep-drugged candidates, still aching from the previous day, hump their Bergens and rifles on to the trucks which will drop them off at intervals in the hills. They will not finish until late that evening, when there is just enough time to tumble into bed for three or four hours. What were termed 'sickeners' used to be built into the course: for example, when the men arrived at the final rendezvous for the day they would see the trucks driving off. They were then told there had been a mistake and they must march another 16 km (10 miles), which inevitably caused a few waverers to jack it in. Those who simply carried on without grumbling would discover that the trucks were actually parked only 1.5 km (1 mile) or so away. More recently, the emphasis has been on encouraging trainees to pass rather than trying to put them off.

By the beginning of the third week, which is known as test week, the intake has probably been roughly halved as more and more red lines are drawn through the faces on the board in the Training Wing. During test week, the candidates have to swim naked across the River Wye carrying their rifles, Bergens and clothes, as well as ascending and descending the fearsome mountain known as Pen-y-Fan, three times non-stop. This is known as the 'Fan Dance'. Nearly 915 m (3,000 feet) high, it is a formidable obstacle for an experienced fell walker to climb once, but three times with a loaded Bergen weighing by that stage around 18 kg (40 lb), a rifle that has no sling and has to be carried all the time and ammunition pouches, calls for a very special type of endurance. To finish the course within the set time limit a candidate has to jog wherever possible, uphill and down. An added refinement is that they will be on their own against the elements, without the companionship and mutual support of a four-man patrol.

The final endurance march is known as 'Long Drag', and those who embark upon it are already half dead from the exhaustion of the previous days. It entails covering a distance of 64 km (40 miles) in 20 hours over some of the most difficult terrain possible, loaded up with 25 kg (55 lb) in the Bergen. To complete it, a candidate has to keep going all the time, stopping only to snatch some high-energy food. More potential recruits will drop out during the course of the ordeal. In February 1979 there was a well-known death: that of Mike Kealey, the hero of Mirbat. He had returned to 22 SAS as a major to command a squadron and opted to put himself through the selection process to prove that he was still up to scratch after a period of deskwork. The weather was appalling, with driving snow, high winds and sleeting rain, yet Kealey opted to march in light order without a layer of windproof clothing, and carrying a Bergen weighted with bricks. This resulted in hypothermia as his normal clothing became soaked with rain and drained away his body heat. A couple of hours into the march, some of those on the course noticed that he had slowed down, yet as they decided to seek shelter lower down the hillside, he was seen on a route which he knew well. Others encountered him from time to time, his condition worsening, and finally, after seven hours of exposure, he was discovered, only just alive by a captain and a corporal. The latter dug a snow hole and tried to use his own body temperature to keep Kealey warm, while the captain went down the hill to get help. Kealey died of hypothermia and it took hours for rescue parties to find him. Suspicions were raised about the cause of his death in a sensational book by the explorer, Sir Ranulph Fiennes, *The Feather Men* (Bloomsbury, 1991).

Long Drag is a fearsome ordeal even for the fittest of candidates. You are on your own, with map, compass, watch and a memorized map reference which you must not forget. Every loss of direction means extra distance to be covered, and if the mist sweeps in, you have to trust your compass. At that stage there is still a competitive edge among the remaining trainees and a great urge to beat any officers who are on the course. Michael Asher, who passed through as a Territorial volunteer, described each pace as like, 'sitting in a fridge with a hundred-pound barbell on my back'. His book, *Shoot to Kill* (Viking, 1990), contains a penetrating description of the whole selection process during the 1970s:

> I can try to replace myself on that last hill, already far beyond the normal bounds of exhaustion, still alone after trekking through snow and wind for almost a day. My feet are a raw and bubbling mass of blisters, especially where my pinched toes have rubbed together, despite the gauze inside my boots. I dare not stop to remove the boots, since I know that my tortured feet will instantly swell up like sausages and I will never be able to get them on again. If I sit down and rest, I may just fade off into unconsciousness and be found the next morning frozen to the ground. There are deep galls on my shoulder now and around the kidneys where the Bergen has rubbed against the flesh like sandpaper. The sweat is cold under my shirt, but I dare not stop to put on my sweater. The heavy wool will draw more precious salt out of my pores and slow me down more rapidly. My feet, hands and face are raw with cold. I might be alone in this shapeless

night. Perhaps everyone else has reached the RV hours ago. Time is running out. Perhaps my bearing is wrong. A wild blackness of hysteria and misery waits to engulf me.

Continuation training

For the lucky few there are the trucks waiting at the end and helping hands from the instructors to ease Bergens from aching shoulders. Mugs of hot sweet tea and cigarettes are passed around. Most sleep in the jolting wagons all the way back to Hereford, knowing that their reward is a long weekend at home. The initial selection has weeded out many, and those who return for continuation training know full well that they are still only there on sufferance.

Continuation training lasts for about four months, and since many of the candidates come from specialist branches of the army, they have to be taught the basic infantry skills, including advanced weapon training and tactical movement. There is also a week each of medical knowledge, signals procedures and demolitions to be passed, interspersed with initiative tests and the ever-present need to keep fit. All this time the candidate is constantly being watched: part of the aim is to weed out anyone who was fit enough to get through the basic selection period but is an idiot when it comes to using their brains. Skills training is followed by a lengthy spell of combat survival and resistance to interrogation.

Combat survival involves learning about edible plants, how to skin and prepare animals and to live off the land by eating fungi, seaweed and roots. It is all about being hunted by others, hiding and camouflage. The basic skills today are refinements of those learned during the Second World War by aircrew who managed to escape. The trainees learn how to deal with dogs and how to move through country while at the same time covering their tracks. For the final exercise they are let loose after a thorough body search, with nothing but their basic clothing. Their task is to make their way to a rendezvous through countryside infested with other soldiers out looking for them. If caught, they will be taken to the 'pen' and interrogated; and if they make it they will suffer the same fate anyway. The basic techniques of interrogation were learned in Western armies from men who were captured during the Korean War and others who were later prisoners of the Vietcong. The techniques that are practised on SAS trainees are those which were condemned by international courts when used on suspects in Northern Ireland. A man who is captured must be able to resist as long as possible in order not to compromise the operation he is on or the lives of his mates who may still be at large, so the exercise must be realistic.

As the essential tool of the interrogator is sensory deprivation, the captives are kept hooded and bound with no means of knowing what the time is, or even which day it is. They are permitted to reveal only their name, rank service number and date of birth. Even an innocent 'Yes' or 'No' can mean failure. The interrogator will offer inducements, such as cigarettes, food or comforting words, and will try to appear as a friend. Alternatively they may threaten a beating, or worse. The captive, who may be stripped naked to increase the sense of humiliation, will be kept for long periods spread-eagled against a wall he can touch only with his fingertips and on tiptoe, which is extremely painful. If he slackens his position, he will be kicked or given a thumping. He has to maintain that position for hours on end while he can sense his guards drinking beer, and smell plates of bacon and eggs. All the while he is subjected to constant 'white noise'. He may well hear sounds of snarling dogs or someone being beaten and screaming. In fact, no real brutality is used as that is felt to be counterproductive, but some of the toughest of candidates have failed at the interrogation stage, subjected to the tender mercies of skilled professionals from the Intelligence Corps who learned their trade in Northern Ireland.

The interrogation is reckoned by many to be the nastiest experience of the whole course, and it is followed by six weeks of learning basic jungle skills in Borneo: tracking through the forests, mounting ambushes and mastering survival in a strange environment. The final stage is completion of the basic army parachuting course.

Having successfully completed selection and continuation training, the handful of remaining candidates are called before the commanding officer and given their beige beret and badge, which means that they are members of the Regiment, having fulfilled all the basic requirements.

Michael Asher, the thinking ex-Para, summed up his experience which might well be that of any SAS man, regular or Territorial:

> No, you can never quite recapture it in words. And to say you walked such and such a distance, carrying such and such a weight conveys nothing. Whenever subsequently I have tried to explain in a few words the agony of SAS selection, and why these marches on the hills should be the basis for choosing members of the best unit of its kind in the world, my words have evoked responses like, "That doesn't sound much!" … SAS selection is one of those things which "doesn't sound much" until you try it. Like the SAS itself, it is simple, direct and deadly effective. But pain and agony fade quickly to become dim memories and pleasure alone remains. I can only say this: some of the strongest, most

determined, most resilient men I have ever met were SAS, and I never found a single one amongst them who found selection easy.

The newly badged members are then assigned to a squadron and can opt for their specializations, both troop and individual, on the basis that they are still virtual beginners. It is said that it takes two full years of hard graft to train an SAS recruit, who will spend the rest of their time with the regiment still training. One of the corruptions of the SAS motto is – 'Who trains, wins!'

Those deciding on free-fall parachuting go on a series of courses which equip them to drop from 7,620 m (25,000 feet) into a low-level canopy opening – the HALO (high altitude low opening) technique. They have to be able to free-fall into a narrow Norwegian valley while presenting a minute radar image, loaded with their kit, and land ready to move off instantly. The mountain troops will be taught the techniques of climbing on rock and ice anywhere in the world, plus the peculiarities of warfare in that environment. The boat troop volunteers will train with the SBS in all the various specialities of amphibious warfare – exiting from submarines and landing craft, navigating Gemini inflatables on to beaches, placing underwater charges, and swimming with breathing apparatus. For mobility troop members it is off to the deserts of the Gulf sheikhdoms to learn the skills of navigating their Land Rovers with the sun compasses, extricating the vehicles from sand dunes, and surviving in the aridity of the sun-baked landscape.

If that were not enough, the newly badged member must also master their own personal skill within the four-man patrol module. Some will learn advanced signalling with the latest sophisticated equipment, while the medics even have to master basic surgery in the field, studying in hospitals. Those with a talent for languages find themselves back at school dealing with the grammar of Malay dialects, different versions of Arabic and today, one could conjecture, Serbo-Croat. The fourth member is the weapons and demolition specialist who will learn to deal with every conceivable firearm, both British and foreign, and will have to pass through the Close Quarters Battle (CQB) wing.

Having mastered the skills necessary to become accepted as a fully trained member of their squadron and troop, after about two years the 'new boy' will settle down to the routine of duty CRW squadron, tours in the trouble-spot of the moment, trips abroad and further individual training. Each member must study the rudiments of the specialities of the others, so that if one is injured the others can carry on. There are also cross-postings between squadrons so that the boat troop recruit has a chance to gain experience in mountaineering or desert navigation. A fully trained SAS recruit is a true all-rounder in every sense of the word.

abbreviations

BAOR	British Army of the Rhine
BATT	British Army Training Teams
CCO	Clandestine Communist Organization (Borneo)
CIA	Central Intelligence Agency
CLF	Commander Land Forces
COBRA	Cabinet Office Briefing Room
CQB	close quarter battle
CRW	counter-revolutionary warfare
CTs	Communist terrorists (Malaya)
DL/AW	Directorate of Land/Air Warfare
DLF	Dhofar Liberation Front
DSL	Defence Systems Ltd
DZ	dropping zone
GSG9	*Grenzschutzgruppe 9*
GIGN	Group d'Intervention de la Gendarmerie Nationale
GPMG	general-purpose machine gun
HALO	high altitude low opening
HE	higher establishment
Int.	Intelligence
Int and Sy	Intelligence and Security Group (Northern Ireland)
JOC	Joint Operations Centre (MoD)
JRRU	Joint Reserve Reconnaissance Unit

KAS	security company founded by Sir David Stirling
KMS	Keeni-Meeni Services Ltd
LRDG	Long Range Desert Group
MEHQ	Middle East Headquarters
MRF	Military Reconnaissance Force (Northern Ireland)
NCO	non-commissioned officer
OCTU	Officer Cadet Training Unit
OP	observation post
PFLO	Popular Front for the Liberation of Oman
PFLP	Popular Front for the Liberation of Palestine
PIRA	Provisional Irish Republican Army
REME	Royal Electrical and Mechanical Engineers
RFA	Royal Fleet Auxiliary
RHQ	Regimental Headquarters
RTU	return to unit
RUC	Royal Ulster Constabulary
SAF	Sultan's Armed Forces (Oman)
SAS	British Special Air Service Regiment
SBS	Special Boat Section
SIS	Secret Intelligence Service (MI6)
SLR	self-loading rifle
SRS	Special Raiding Squadron
SOAF	Sultan of Oman's Air Force
SOE	Special Operations Executive
SSM	Squadron Sergeant Major
TA	Territorial Army

taking it further

Further reading

The Second World War, 1940–5

General histories: the SAS

Geraghty, Tony, *Who Dares Wins*, Arms & Armour Press, 1980; the Fontana paperback edition 1983, has an additional chapter on the Falklands.
— *This is the SAS – A Photographic History*, Arms & Armour Press, 1982.

Ladd, James D., *SAS Operations*, Robert Hale, 1986.

Macdonald, Peter, *The SAS in Action*, Sidgwick & Jackson, 1990.

Seymour, William, *British Special Forces*, Grafton Books, 1985.

Shortt, J., *The Special Air Service*, Men-at-Arms Series No. 116, Osprey, 1981.

Strawson, John, *A History of the SAS Regiment*, Secker & Warburg, 1984.

Warner, Phillip, *The SAS*, William Kimber, 1971; Sphere Books paperback edition 1983.

General histories: the SBS

Courtney, G. B., *SBS in World War Two*, Robert Hale, 1983.

Ladd, James D., *SBS: The Invisible Raiders*, Arms & Armour Press, 1983.

Pitt, Barrie, *Special Boat Squadron*, Century, 1983.

Warner, Phillip, *The SBS*, Sphere Books, 1983.

Biographies

Bradford, Roy, and Dillon, Martin, *Rogue Warrior of the SAS*, John Murray, 1987.

Cowles, Virginia, *The Phantom Major*, Collins, 1955.

Marrinan, Patrick, *Colonel Paddy*, Ulster Press, 1960.

First-person accounts

Appleyard, E., *'Geoffrey'*, Blandford Press, 1947.

Byrne, J. V., *The General Salutes a Soldier*, Robert Hale, 1986.

Challenor, Tanky, with Draper, Alfred, *SAS and the Met*, Leo Cooper, 1990.

Cooper, John, with Kemp, Anthony, *One of the 'Originals'*, Pan, 1991.

De Souza, Ken, *Escape from Ascoli*, Newton, Publications, 1990.

Dumford-Slater, John, *Commando*, William Kimber, 1953.

Farran, Roy, *Winged Dagger*, Collins, 1948; reissued by Arms & Armour Press, 1986.

— *Operation Tombola*, Collins, 1960; reissued by Arms & Armour Press, 1986.

Harrison, D. I., *These Men are Dangerous*, Cassell, 1957.

Hills, R. T., *Phantom Was There*, Edward Arnold, 1951.

Hislop, John, *Anything but a Soldier*, Michael Joseph, 1965.

Hughes, J. Quentin, *Who Cares Who Wins*, privately published, 1989.

Johnston, Charles, *Mo, and Other Originals*, Hamish Hamilton, 1971.

James [Pleydell], Malcolm, *Born of the Desert*, Collins, 1945.

Maclean, Fitzroy, *Eastern Approaches*, Jonathan Cape, 1949.

McLuskey, Fraser, *Parachute Padre*, SCM Press, 1951.

Newby, Eric, *Love and War in the Apennines*, Picador, 1983.

Pringle, Jack, *Colditz Last Stop*, William Kimber, 1988.

Sykes, Christopher, *Four Studies in Loyalty*, Collins, 1946.

Verney, John, *A Dinner of Herbs*, Collins, 1966.

— *Going to the Wars*, Collins, 1955; reissued in paperback by Anthony Mott, 1983.

Vaculik, Serge, *Air Commando*, Jarrolds, 1954.

Waugh, Evelyn, *The Letters of Evelyn Waugh*, ed. Mark Amory, Penguin, 1982.

Young, Irene, *Enigma Variations*, Mainstream, 1990.

The Long Range Desert Group

Constable, Trevor, *Hidden Heroes*, Arthur Barker, 1971.

Crichton-Stuart, Michael, *G Patrol*, William Kimber, 1958.

Kennedy-Shaw, W. B., *Long Range Desert Group*, Collins, 1945.

Lloyd-Owen, David, *Providence Their Guide*, Harrap, 1980.

— *The Desert My Dwelling Place*, Cassell, 1957; reissued by Arms & Armour Press, 1986.

Secondary sources

Boehm, Boettcher, Reuter and Weingardt, *Sicherungslager Rotenfels, Ein Konzentrationslager in Deutschland*, Suddeutscher Paedogogische Verlag, Ludwigsburg, 1989.

Buxton, David, *Honour to the Airborne*, Part 2, Elmdon Publishing, Solihull, 1985.

Calmette, A., *Les Equipes Jedburgh dans la Bataille de France*, Paris, 1966.

Chouette, La, *La Resistance dans la Vienne*, privately published.

Cooper, Artemis, *Cairo in the War*, Hamish Hamilton, 1989.

Deighton, Len, *et al.*, *Alamein and the Desert War*, Sphere Books, 1967.

Flamand, Col. Roger, *L'inconnu du French Squadron*, privately published, 1983.

Foot, M. R. D., *SOE in France*, HMSO, 1966.

Hastings, Max, *Das Reich*, Michael Joseph, 1981.

Kemp, Anthony, *The Secret Hunters*, Michael O'Mara Books, 1986.

Lewis, Laurence, *Echoes of Resistance*, Costello, 1985.

Marnais, A. (ed.), *L'Odyssee des Parachutistes SAS du Capitaine Tonkin et des Maquisards du Capitaine Dieudonne*, privately published.

Racault, Gaston, *La Vienne pendant la Seconde Guerre Mondiale: Vol. 3, Les Maquis, la Liberation*, CRDP, Poitiers, 1987.

Ricatte, Rene, *Viombois, haut lieu de la Resistance*, GMA-Vosges, 1984.

Rousselet, Maurice, *Occupation et liberation d'un coin de Bourgogne*, privately published, 1980.

Swinson, Arthur, *The Raiders*, Pan, 1968.

Warner, Phillip, *Phantom*, Kimber, 1982.

The post-war era

Adams, James, *Secret Armies*, Hutchinson, 1988.

Adams, James, Morgan, Robin, and Bambridge, Anthony, *Ambush. The War between the SAS and the IRA*, Pan, 1988.

Akehurst, John, *We Won a War: The Campaign in Oman 1965–75*, Michael Russell, 1982.

Arkless, David C., *The Secret War. Dhoftr, 1971–72*, William Kimber, 1988.

Asher, Michael, *Shoot to Kill*, Viking, 1990.

Ballinger, Adam, *The Quiet Soldier*, Chapman, 1992.

Barber, Noel, *War of the Running Dogs: Malaya 1948–1960*, Collins, 1971.

Billière, Gen. Sir Peter de la, *Storm Command*, Collins, 1992.

— *Looking for trouble*, HarperCollins, 1994.

Burden, R. A., *et al.*, *The Air War*, Arms & Armour Press, 1986.

Cole, Barbara, *The Elite: The Story of the Rhodesian Special Air Service*, Three Knights, Transkei, 1985.

— *The Elite – Pictorial*, Three Knights, 1987. Photographic supplement to *The Elite*.

Cooper, Johnny (with Anthony Kemp), *One of the Originals*, Pan, 1991.

Cramer, Chris and Harris, Sim, *Hostage*, John Clare, 1982.

Daly, Lt.-Col. Ron Reid, *Selous Scouts. Top Secret War*, Galligo, South Africa, 1982.

Deane-Drummond, Anthony, *Arrows of Fortune*, Leo Cooper, 1992.

Dewar, Michael, *The British Army in Northern Ireland*, Arms & Armour Press, 1985.

Dickens, Peter, *SAS: The Jungle Campaign – 22 Special Air Service Regiment in Borneo*, Arms & Armour Press, 1983.

Dillon, Martin, *The Dirty War*, Hutchinson, 1990.

Fiennes, Sir Ranulph, *The Feather Men*, Bloomsbury, 1991.

— *Living Dangerously*, Macmillan, 1987.

— *Where Soldiers Fear to Tread*, Hodder & Stoughton, 1975.

Fleming, J. and Faux, R., *Soldiers on Everest*, HMSO, 1977.

Fox, Robert, *Eyewitness Falklands*, Methuen, 1982.

Hastings, Max and Jenkins, Simon, *The Battle of the Falklands*, Michael Joseph, 1983.

Hoe, Alan, *David Stirling*, Little, Brown, 1992.

Horner, D. M., *Phantoms of the Jungle*, Unwin, 1989; Greenhill Books, 1991.

Jeapes, A. S., *SAS: Operation Oman*, William Kimber, 1980.

Kemp, Anthony, *The Secret Hunters*, Michael O'Mara Books, 1986.

— *The SAS Savage Wars of Peace*, John Murray, 1993.

Kennedy, Michael Paul, *Soldier 'I' SAS*, Bloomsbury, 1989.

Kitson, Frank, *Bunch of Fives*, Faber & Faber, 1977.

Large, Lofty, *One Man's Special Air Service*, William Kimber, 1987.

Macdonald, Peter, *The SAS in Action*, Sidgwick & Jackson, 1990.

McManners, Hugh, *Falklands Commando*, William Kimber, 1984.

McNab, Andy, *Bravo Two Zero*, Bantam Press, 1993.

Murray, Raymond, *The SAS in Ireland*, Mercier Press, Cork, 1990.

Niven, D. M., *Special Men, Special War. Portraits of Dhofar*, privately published.

Philip, Craig and Taylor, Allan, *Inside the SAS*, Bloomsbury, 1993.

Rennie, Frank, *Regular Soldier*, Endeavour Press, Auckland, 1987.

Rivers, Gayle, *The Specialist*, Guild, 1985.

Seale, P. and McConville, M., *The Hilton Assignment*, Temple Smith, 1973.

Smiley, David and Kemp, Peter, *Arabian Assignment*, Leo Cooper, 1975.

Stokes, Brummie, *Soldiers and Sherpas*, Michael Joseph, 1988.

Strawson, John, *A History of the SAS Regiment*, Seeker & Warburg, 1984.

Sunday Times 'Insight' Team, *Siege*, Hamlyn paperback edition, 1986.

Thompson, Leroy, *The Rescuers. The World's Top Anti-Terrorist Units*, Paladin, 1986.

Urban, Mark, *Big Boys' Rules*, Faber & Faber, 1992.

Vaux, Nick, *March to the South Atlantic*, Buchan & Enright, 1986.

Wiseman, John, *The Official SAS Survival Handbook*, Collins Harvill, 1986.

the cold war
0340 884940 £8.99

nazi germany
0340 884908 £8.99

the middle east
0340 884916 £8.99

the second world war
0340 884932 £8.99

special forces
0340 884924 £8.99

the first world war
0340 884894 £8.99

the cold war

teach
yourself

c. b. jones

- Understand the period that gave us the Cuban crisis, the Berlin wall, nuclear weapons and James Bond
- Discover more about this hidden conflict
- Read a compelling guide to this 45-year-long war

teach yourself the cold war is an accessible introduction to a war that shaped the latter half of the twentieth century. It covers all aspects, from questioning whether the tension really ended with the fall of the Berlin wall, to examining what JFK and his assassin had in common. Understand the global reach of this hidden conflict and its effects on the world in recent history and today.

C. B. Jones is an experienced teacher and Head of Faculty. She is also an A Level examiner with a specialist knowledge of twentieth century history.

teach
yourself

the second world war
alan farmer

- Explore the events of the Second World War
- Discover its impact on those involved
- Understand the reasons behind the conflict and who was to blame

teach yourself the second world war is an accessible introduction to one of the most important, tragic and costly events in history. This war had an unimaginable impact on the entire world, causing the deaths of over 50 million people. Follow the main military campaigns of the war, discover how it affected the countries involved and develop your understanding of why the Allied powers were able to achieve victory.

Alan Farmer is Head of History at St Martin's College, Lancaster and has written a large number of books on modern American, European and British history.

the first world war
david evans

- Gain a better understanding of key events during the First World War
- Discover the reasons behind the conflict
- Gain an insight into the experiences of those involved

teach yourself the first world war is a compelling introduction to a conflict on a scale never experienced in the world before. When war broke out in 1914 some predicted that it would be 'over by Christmas', yet four years later, following the slaughter of over nine million men, still no peace had been made. This book considers the roles of the leading politicians and explores the impact on the civilians and societies involved.

David Evans is an established writer and lecturer. He has written over twenty books covering aspects of modern European history and is a contributor on both television and radio.

nazi germany
michael lynch

- Discover this extraordinary period
- Understand the motives of the individuals who created and led the Nazi movement
- Gain an insight into the experiences of those involved

teach yourself nazi germany is an accessible introduction to one of the most controversial periods in modern history. The years 1933–45 witnessed the take-over of Germany by a man and a movement whose racial and political policies are now regarded with universal abhorrence. Yet in all of European history there has never been a more genuinely popular regime than that of the Nazis. This book immerses you in the remarkable Third Reich story and the controversies that still surround it.

Michael Lynch is a tutor at the University of Leicester and is also a writer, specializing in modern European and Asian history.

teach
yourself

the middle east since 1945
stewart ross

- Read an accessible guide to today's political hotspot
- Understand the development of the region
- Discover more about a major world issue

teach yourself the middle east since 1945 tells the story of the modern world's most troubled region. It is lively yet authoritative, examining the origin and developments of issues that have made the headlines over the last half century. This book addresses many questions about the region, including why the Israeli–Palestinian conflict has lasted so long and the background to the two Gulf Wars and presents each aspect with engaging objectivity.

Stewart Ross taught in a variety of institutions worldwide before becoming a writer, lecturer and broadcaster. He has written over 175 books, including widely acclaimed historical works.

teach yourself ®

Hinduism
History, 101 Key Ideas
How to Win at Horse Racing
How to Win at Poker
HTML Publishing on the WWW
Human Anatomy & Physiology
Hungarian
Icelandic
Indian Head Massage
Indonesian
Information Technology, 101 Key Ideas
Internet, The
Irish
Islam
Italian
Italian, Beginner's
Italian Grammar
Italian Grammar, Quick Fix
Italian, Instant
Italian, Improve your
Italian Language, Life & Culture
Italian Verbs
Italian Vocabulary
Japanese
Japanese, Beginner's
Japanese, Instant
Japanese Language, Life & Culture
Japanese Script, Beginner's
Java
Jewellery Making
Judaism
Korean
Latin
Latin American Spanish
Latin, Beginner's
Latin Dictionary
Latin Grammar
Letter Writing Skills
Linguistics
Linguistics, 101 Key Ideas
Literature, 101 Key Ideas
Mahjong
Managing Stress
Marketing
Massage
Mathematics
Mathematics, Basic
Media Studies
Meditation
Mosaics
Music Theory
Needlecraft
Negotiating
Nepali

Norwegian
Origami
Panjabi
Persian, Modern
Philosophy
Philosophy of Mind
Philosophy of Religion
Philosophy of Science
Philosophy, 101 Key Ideas
Photography
Photoshop
Physics
Piano
Planets
Planning Your Wedding
Polish
Politics
Portuguese
Portuguese, Beginner's
Portuguese Grammar
Portuguese, Instant
Portuguese Language, Life & Culture
Postmodernism
Pottery
Powerpoint 2002
Presenting for Professionals
Project Management
Psychology
Psychology, 101 Key Ideas
Psychology, Applied
Quark Xpress
Quilting
Recruitment
Reflexology
Reiki
Relaxation
Retaining Staff
Romanian
Russian
Russian, Beginner's
Russian Grammar
Russian, Instant
Russian Language, Life & Culture
Russian Script, Beginner's
Sanskrit
Screenwriting
Serbian
Setting up a Small Business
Shorthand, Pitman 2000
Sikhism
Spanish
Spanish, Beginner's
Spanish Grammar
Spanish Grammar, Quick Fix

Spanish, Instant
Spanish, Improve your
Spanish Language, Life & Culture
Spanish Starter Kit
Spanish Verbs
Spanish Vocabulary
Speaking on Special Occasions
Speed Reading
Statistical Research
Statistics
Swahili
Swahili Dictionary
Swedish
Tagalog
Tai Chi
Tantric Sex
Teaching English as a Foreign Language
Teaching English One to One
Teams and Team-Working
Thai
Time Management
Tracing your Family History
Travel Writing
Trigonometry
Turkish
Turkish, Beginner's
Typing
Ukrainian
Urdu
Urdu Script, Beginner's
Vietnamese
Volcanoes
Watercolour Painting
Weight Control through Diet and Exercise
Welsh
Welsh Dictionary
Welsh Language, Life & Culture
Wills and Probate
Wine Tasting
Winning at Job Interviews
Word 2002
World Faiths
Writing a Novel
Writing for Children
Writing Poetry
Xhosa
Yoga
Zen
Zulu